PRACTICE
MAKES
PERFECT™

Pre-Algebra

WITHDRAWN

**PRACTICE
MAKES
PERFECT™**

Pre-Algebra

Erin Muschla-Berry

Mc
Graw
Hill

New York Chicago San Francisco Lisbon London Madrid Mexico City
Milan New Delhi San Juan Seoul Singapore Sydney Toronto

1 2 3 4 5 6 7 8 9 10 11 12 13 14 15 16 17   QDB/QDB   1 9 8 7 6 5 4 3 2

ISBN   978-0-07-177278-5
MHID   0-07-177278-2

e-ISBN 978-0-07-178128-2
e-MHID   0-07-178128-5

Library of Congress Control Number 2011915001

McGraw-Hill, the McGraw-Hill Publishing logo, Practice Makes Perfect, and related trade dress are trademarks or registered trademarks of The McGraw-Hill Companies and/or its affiliates in the United States and other countries and may not be used without written permission. All other trademarks are the property of their respective owners. The McGraw-Hill Companies is not associated with any product or vendor mentioned in this book.

Interior design by Village Bookworks, Inc.

McGraw-Hill products are available at special quantity discounts to use as premiums and sales promotions or for use in corporate training programs. To contact a representative, please e-mail us at bulksales@mcgraw-hill.com.

This book is printed on acid-free paper.

Contents

3 Patterns, expressions, equations, and inequalities   55

About this book

Success in upper-level mathematics courses is dependent on the foundation a student receives in algebra. Success in algebra is dependent on the math skills that students learn in pre-algebra. *Practice Makes Perfect: Pre-Algebra* is a useful resource for learning the skills necessary for success in pre-algebra, while also providing prerequisite skills for success in algebra. This book contains lessons, examples, and exercises of practice problems on pre-algebra topics.

Students, their parents, and teachers will find this book useful. Students may work independently, or with their parents, on the concepts and skills presented in the book. They may use the material for extra practice or enrichment. Teachers may supplement their lessons and activities with the examples and practice problems.

Pre-algebra encompasses a wide range of topics and is often difficult for students to master. However, with additional practice and support, every student can master the pre-algebra concepts and skills necessary to achieve success in math.

How to use this book

Practice Makes Perfect: Pre-Algebra is divided into five chapters. Each chapter includes several lessons on major topics with detailed explanations, examples, and exercises containing practice problems. An answer key is provided at the end of the book.

In Chapter 1, "The basics: numbers and properties," you will learn basic number sense and number theory. This chapter includes 6 lessons and 7 exercises that focus on classifying numbers, using a number line, comparing and ordering numbers, and the properties of numbers.

Chapter 2, "Operations with rational numbers," includes 17 lessons and 28 exercises that focus on addition, subtraction, multiplication, and division of rational numbers. This chapter also includes the order of operations, operations with exponents, and squares and square roots.

Chapter 3, "Patterns, expressions, equations, and inequalities," serves as an introduction to algebra. It includes 16 lessons and 30 exercises that focus on finding patterns, evaluating expressions, and solving equations and inequalities.

Chapter 4, "Graphing," includes 8 lessons and 15 exercises. This chapter focuses on graphing equations and inequalities on a number line and graphing points and equations in a coordinate plane.

Chapter 5, "Functions," focuses on the domains, ranges, and rules of functions, represented in tables and equations. It includes 4 lessons and 7 exercises.

Each lesson begins with an explanation of a concept and contains examples and step-by-step instructions for solving problems. Most lessons are followed by two sets of practice problems, with the first being self-correcting. Each self-correcting exercise contains easy-to-follow directions and requires no additional materials. By completing the exercise, you will finish a statement or uncover an interesting fact.

To get the most from this book, always read the explanation of a lesson and study the examples before beginning an exercise. If you need help once you start an exercise, refer back to the lesson and examples. When you are done, be sure to check your answers against the answer key. For any problems in which you made a mistake, double-check your work. Finding and understanding mistakes is a key to mastering concepts and skills.

This book offers a total of 51 lessons and 87 practice exercises. These lessons and exercises provide a vast amount of material that will help you as you begin, practice, and master pre-algebra concepts and skills. With hard work and practice, you will gain the required knowledge for learning algebra.

Pre-Algebra

The basics: numbers and properties

Classifying numbers: rational, natural, whole, integer, irrational

Mathematics is a language of numbers. Although many people think of numbers simply as numbers, mathematicians have classified numbers in a variety of ways. Classifying numbers helps you organize numbers and that, in turn, helps you organize your mathematical reasoning.

Natural numbers, also known as counting numbers, begin at 1 and continue forever. Each number is one more than the previous number. All natural numbers are positive numbers. An easy way to remember the set of natural numbers is to remember that they are the counting numbers: 1, 2, 3 . . .

Whole numbers are the set of natural numbers and zero. The set of whole numbers begins with zero and continues: 0, 1, 2, 3 . . . Remember that the word *whole* has an "o" in it. This "o" can help you remember that the set of whole numbers begins with "0." All natural numbers are whole numbers, but not all whole numbers are natural numbers. Zero is a whole number but not a natural number.

Integers are the set of natural numbers, their opposites, and zero. For example, 1 and –1 are opposites. This set includes: . . . –3, –2, –1, 0, 1, 2, 3 . . . The " . . . " are ellipses and indicate that the set continues infinitely in both directions. All natural and whole numbers are integers, but not all integers are whole or natural numbers. The opposites of whole numbers, for example –1, –2, –3, are only classified as integers.

Rational numbers include natural numbers, whole numbers, integers, fractions, terminating decimals, and repeating decimals. A rational number is defined as a number that can be represented as the quotient of two integers or stated algebraically as $\frac{a}{b}$, where a and b are integers and $b \neq 0$. The symbol $\neq$ means is not equal to. For example, 2 is a rational number because it can be expressed as $\frac{2}{1}$. $-0.\bar{3}$ is a rational number because it can be expressed as $-\frac{1}{3}$. (The bar, or repetend, above a digit or group of digits shows that the digit or group of digits repeats indefinitely. Such numbers are rational numbers.)

Irrational numbers are a separate category of numbers that cannot be expressed as the quotient of two integers. Irrational numbers are numbers that can be expressed as decimals that neither terminate nor repeat. The history of the term *irrational* dates back to ancient Greece when mathematicians believed all numbers were rational. But the Pythagoreans, a society of mathematicians, proved

1

in the 6th century B.C. that $\sqrt{2}$ could not be expressed as a fraction. They called $\sqrt{2}$ and similar numbers irrational.

Both irrational numbers and rational numbers are subsets of the set of *real numbers*. All rational and irrational numbers are real and are included in the set of real numbers.

Following is a graphic organizer that provides a visual representation of the number system.

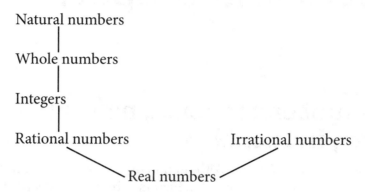

If a number is classified in one category, it automatically also belongs to the set of numbers shown below it on this graphic organizer. For example, 2 is a natural number. It is also a whole number, an integer, a rational number, and a real number. −3 is an integer, a rational number, and a real number. π, which cannot be expressed as a fraction, is an irrational number and a real number.

EXERCISE 1·1

Circle the number or numbers that do not belong in each category. Place the letter of each circled number in the space above the number at the end of the exercise to complete the sentence. Your answer will tell you something about Pythagoras.

Natural:	−4	11	1	5	−10	0.5	$\frac{19}{20}$	12
	T	D	A	B	E	N	G	Y
Whole:	6	$-\frac{1}{3}$	3	7	−2	13	−5	0.49
	U	T	C	S	A	P	Y	M
Integer:	−5	1	$-\frac{2}{5}$	15	0.7	100	$\frac{7}{8}$	−11
	X	M	R	Z	E	L	R	S
Rational:	$-\frac{1}{4}$	$\frac{1}{\sqrt{3}}$	−0.857	$\frac{15}{20}$	π	74	1.25	$\sqrt{8}$
	J	E	Q	K	A	O	A	O
Irrational:	$\sqrt{2}$	10	$-\frac{2}{3}$	$0.\overline{1}$	$\sqrt{3}$	7	$\sqrt{11}$	1.618...
	U	H	P	H	K	O	I	O
Real:	$\frac{8}{5}$	$-\frac{1}{5}$	8	50	$\sqrt{8}$	0.5	−17	$\sqrt{99}$
	K	P	E	V	N	U	L	S

Pythagoras, a mathematician of ancient Greece, is not only known for his work with irrational numbers. He is most famous for proving the

| $-\dfrac{2}{3}$ | -5 | -4 | 10 | -2 | $\dfrac{19}{20}$ | 7 | $-\dfrac{2}{5}$ | 0.7 | π | 0.5 |

| $-\dfrac{1}{3}$ | $0.\overline{1}$ | $\dfrac{1}{\sqrt{3}}$ | $\sqrt{8}$ | $\dfrac{7}{8}$ | -10 | 0.49 |

that describes the relationship between the sides of a right triangle as $a^2 + b^2 = c^2$.

EXERCISE
1·2

Place an X in the appropriate row to indicate where each number is classified. Remember that some numbers may belong to several groups of numbers.

	5	$-\dfrac{2}{3}$	$\sqrt{11}$	0	0.67	-25	$0.\overline{4}$	123	$\dfrac{9}{10}$
Natural									
Whole									
Integer									
Rational									
Irrational									
Real									

	$-\dfrac{3}{13}$	17	$\sqrt{23}$	84	$-\dfrac{25}{26}$	-0.45	-55	π	1
Natural									
Whole									
Integer									
Rational									
Irrational									
Real									

Numbers on the number line

A number line is a line on which all real numbers can be placed, according to their value. It can be a useful tool for understanding the values and relationships of numbers.

A number line showing the set of whole numbers is pictured in Figure 1-1.

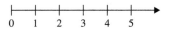

Figure 1-1

Notice that a scale of 1 is used for this number line. Each whole number is one more than the number before it. The spaces between each of the numbers are equal, representing the same increase in value between each two numbers. The arrow shows that the number line increases infinitely.

By extending this number line in the opposite direction as well, the set of integers can be shown (Figure 1-2).

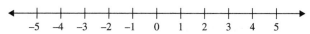

Figure 1-2

A scale of 1 is also used for this number line. Positive numbers are located to the right of zero. Negative numbers are located to the left of zero. The numbers to the left of zero are the opposites of the numbers to the right of zero.

Fractions and decimals can be placed on this number line by dividing the number line into fractional intervals, as shown on the number line below. This makes it possible to show the placement of the fractions or decimals more clearly. Notice that a scale of 0.5 is used in Figure 1-3.

Figure 1-3

The points on the number line represent the graphs of 0.5 and −3.9.

Number lines show the relative value of numbers. A larger number will always be to the right of a smaller number. As you move to the right on the number line, the value of the numbers increases. Moving to the left on the number line shows smaller numbers. For example, 4 is larger than 1 because 4 is farther right on the number line than 1. Similarly, −5 is less than −2 because −5 is farther left on the number line than −2.

Create a number line to graph each set of numbers shown in questions 1–3 below. Then use your number lines to answer questions 4–6.

1. Use a scale of 1 and create a number line to include the integers from −10 to 10. Then graph the points −5, 2, and 9.

2. Use a scale of 0.25 and create a number line to include the rational numbers from 0 to 5. Then graph the points 3.5 and 4.5.

3. Use a scale of $\frac{1}{4}$ and create a number line to include the rational numbers from −4 to 4. Then graph the points: $-3\frac{1}{2}$, $-1\frac{3}{4}$, and 2.

4. Which number is larger, −5 or 2? Why?

5. Which number is smaller, 4.5 or 3.5? Why?

6. Which number is larger, $-3\frac{1}{2}$ or $-1\frac{3}{4}$? Why?

Movement on the number line

Although number lines help determine the relative magnitude of numbers, they also help in determining the relationship of one number to another. They show the distance, or value, from one number to another (Figure 1-4).

Figure 1-4

For example, the number line above shows the set of integers from −5 to 5. Using this number line, questions such as the following can be answered.

- What is the distance between −3 and −1? Start at −3 and count the number of units until you reach −1. You will count −2 and −1. The answer is 2. You do not count −3 as one of the numbers because that is the number you are starting with. The distance is 2.
- Which number is 3 units to the right of 1? Start at 1 and count 3 units to the right. You move right because 3 is a positive number. You will end at 4. 4 is 3 units from 1.
- Which number is 2 less than −2? Begin at −2 and move 2 units to the left. You must move left because the question asks for a value that is "less than." This is a negative change, or subtraction. You must move left because the value is taken away from the starting number. −4 is 2 less than −2.
- What is the opposite of 5? Opposites are defined as two numbers that are the same distance from zero on a number line. A pair of opposites includes one positive and one negative number. −5 is the opposite of 5.

Create number lines to answer the following questions. A sample number line is provided.

1. What is the opposite of −2?

2. Which number is 5 more than 2?

3. Which number is 4 less than −3?

4. What is the distance between 0.5 and 2.5?

5. What number is 3 more than $1\frac{3}{5}$?

6. What number is the opposite of 5.75?

7. What is the distance between −5 and 3?

8. What number is 4 spaces to the left of −2?

9. What number is 4.5 more than −3.5?

10. What number is 6.8 less than 0?

Comparing numbers

An inequality shows that two expressions are not equal. There are several different inequality signs that may be used to show such a relationship.

- The notation $a < b$ means that a is less than b.
- The notation $a > b$ means that a is greater than b.
- The notation $a \leq b$ means that a is less than or equal to b.
- The notation $a \geq b$ means that a is greater than or equal to b.
- The notation $a \neq b$ means that a is not equal to b.

The point of the inequality symbol points to the smaller number in each of the inequalities listed above. Conversely, the opening of the sign opens toward the larger number.

Inequalities are often used to compare real numbers by showing which is larger or smaller. For example, $5 > 3$ shows that 5 is greater than 3; $-4 < -1$ shows that −4 is less than −1. The inequality $2.3 \leq 4.6$ shows that 2.3 is less than or equal to 4.6. When determining which inequality symbol to use, think about the placement of the numbers on a number line. A larger number will always be to the right of a smaller number. When writing inequalities, it may be helpful to create number lines as a visual representation to compare numbers.

Comparing fractions often requires a few more steps than comparing integers and decimals. There are two methods you may use: writing equivalent fractions or converting fractions to decimals.

Example 1: Compare $\dfrac{7}{8}$ and $\dfrac{3}{4}$ by writing equivalent fractions.

Because these fractions have different denominators, you must first find equivalent fractions with the same denominator. The least common denominator of 8 and 4 is 8.

- Express $\dfrac{3}{4}$ as $\dfrac{6}{8}$ because $\dfrac{3}{4} \times \dfrac{2}{2} = \dfrac{6}{8}$.

- Now compare $\dfrac{7}{8}$ and $\dfrac{6}{8}$. Because the denominators are equivalent, only compare the numerators.

- Since 7 is larger than 6, $\dfrac{7}{8} > \dfrac{3}{4}$.

Example 2: Compare $\dfrac{7}{8}$ and $\dfrac{3}{4}$ by converting each fraction into a decimal.

- Change each fraction to a decimal by dividing the numerator by the denominator. $\dfrac{7}{8} = 0.875$ and $\dfrac{3}{4} = 0.75$.

- Compare the decimals. Since 0.875 is larger than 0.75, $\dfrac{7}{8} > \dfrac{3}{4}$.

EXERCISE

1·5

Circle the appropriate symbol to make each statement true. Then match the letter or number under the symbol with the number of the problem at the end of the exercise to complete the sentence.

1. 10 ___ 7

   <   >   =

   7   3   9

2. −3 ___ −1

   <   ≥   >

   A   G   B

3. −2 ___ 0

   ≥   =   <

   K   C   I

4. 21 ___ 22

   ≥   ≠   >

   M   L   W

5. −17 ___ −30

≥	=	<
6	3	5

6. 0.95 ___ 1.2

≤	=	>
B	R	N

7. $\frac{3}{5}$ ___ $-\frac{1}{2}$

>	<	≤
E	M	B

8. $-\frac{4}{5}$ ___ $-\frac{9}{10}$

=	≤	>
G	U	A

9. $-0.\overline{3}$ ___ $-0.\overline{6}$

<	>	≤
Z	Y	R

10. −15.3 ___ −15.7

≤	<	>
P	O	A

11. $\frac{5}{20}$ ___ $\frac{1}{4}$

>	<	=
K	A	I

12. $0.\overline{3}$ ___ $0.\overline{6}$

≥	>	<
8	2	1

13. $-\frac{11}{12}$ ___ $-\frac{9}{10}$

>	=	<
M	N	L

14. 5.75 ___ 5.92

<	>	≥
I	U	E

15. $-\dfrac{3}{4}$ ___ -0.5

        <   =   >

        Z   J   D

16. -0.68 ___ $-\dfrac{4}{5}$

        ≤   >   <

        L   Z   T

The highest temperature ever recorded on Earth was

____ ____ ____ degrees Fahrenheit in
12   1   5

____ ____   ____ ____ ____ ____ ____ ____
7   13   10   16   3   15   11   8

____ ____ ____ ____ ____
4   14   6   9   2   on September 13, 1922.

Ordering numbers

Ordering numbers is another way to compare numbers. Numbers may be listed in ascending or descending order. When numbers are arranged in ascending order, the lowest number begins the set and increases to the highest number in the set. Ascending order is more commonly known as least to greatest. When numbers are arranged in descending order, or greatest to least, the highest number begins the set and decreases to the lowest number in the set.

To order numbers, first determine the value of each number. Think about whether the number is positive or negative, a fraction or decimal. Then think about the relationships between the numbers in the set. It may be helpful to create a number line. By creating a number line and graphing the numbers in the set, you will already have put the numbers in ascending order. Remember to rewrite fractions so that they have the same denominator or change fractions into decimals, if necessary.

Example 1: Write the following in ascending order: 5, –1, 2, –3, 0.

♦ Examine the positive and negative numbers. Since positive numbers are always greater than negative numbers, –1 and –3 are less than the other numbers in the set. –3 is less than –1.
♦ Consider the rest of the numbers. Of 0, 5, and 2, 0 has the least value, followed by 2 and then 5.
♦ Arranged in ascending order, then, the numbers are –3, –1, 0, 2, 5.

Constructing a number line like the one in Figure 1-5 and graphing the numbers shows the order of the numbers.

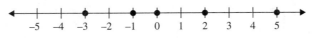

Figure 1-5

Example 2: Write the following in order from greatest to least: $\frac{3}{4}$, $-2\frac{7}{8}$, -3, 1.75, 2.

- Change all the fractions and decimals to fractions with the same denominator or to decimals. In this example, all the fractions are changed to decimals by dividing the numerator by the denominator. $\frac{3}{4} = 0.75$ and $-2\frac{7}{8} = -2.875$.

- Begin with the greatest number, which is 2, and order the numbers in descending order. The positive numbers are 2, 1.75, and $\frac{3}{4}$, or 0.75. As the positive numbers get closer to zero, their value decreases.

- Next, order the negative numbers from greatest to least. $-2\frac{7}{8}$, or -2.875, is larger than -3 because -3 is farther to the left on the number line.

- Arranged in order from greatest to least, then, the numbers are 2, 1.75, $\frac{3}{4}$, $-2\frac{7}{8}$, -3.

Note that you may also create a number line and graph the numbers as pictured in Figure 1-6.

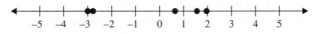

Figure 1-6

The graph shows the numbers arranged from least to greatest (reading from left to right). Reversing the order of the numbers places them in descending order.

Place each set of numbers in order according to the directions. Then write the letter of the fourth number in each set above the number of the problem at the end of the exercise to complete the sentence.

PLACE EACH SET BELOW IN ORDER
FROM LEAST TO GREATEST

1. 0, 3, −2, −3, −5

   R   I   B   Q   P

3. 10, −10, 1, 0, −19

   O   C   U   P   K

5. −67, −75, −101, −212, −80

   L   T   N   K   D

7. $\dfrac{9}{10}, \dfrac{4}{5}, -\dfrac{15}{20}, -\dfrac{4}{16}, -1$

   Y   N   R   B   L

9. −2, −1.9, −2.3, −1, −1.8

   J   S   C   M   V

11. $-\dfrac{17}{18}, -0.95, -0.96, -1, -\dfrac{6}{7}$

   S   T   R   M   P

PLACE EACH SET BELOW IN ORDER
FROM GREATEST TO LEAST

2. 15, 21, 14, 25, 18

   T   U   Z   M   E

4. −7, 2, 3, −5, −2

   W   A   O   E   L

6. 20, 18, 19, 18.5, 17.5,

   R   M   H   A   O

8. −10.9, −11.2, −11.$\overline{2}$, −11.1 , −11

   P   E   O   I   W

10. $1\dfrac{3}{5}, 2\dfrac{5}{7}, -3, 1, 3\dfrac{1}{3}$

   F   A   Y   O   H

12. 1.$\overline{9}$, 1.99, 2, 1.9, 2.01

   A   E   Y   L   J

___ ___ ___ ___ ___
6   10   3   7   2

___ ___ ___ ___ ___ ___ ___
12 9 4 1 8 11 5

is the world's highest mountain with an elevation of 8,850 meters (29,035 feet).

Associative, commutative, and identity properties

Mathematicians have summarized many properties of numbers. The commutative and associative properties are two properties that show how to compute and simplify expressions. Both properties apply to addition and multiplication.

The commutative property states that numbers can be added or multiplied in any order and still equal the same sum or product:

For all real numbers a and b, $a + b = b + a$ and $a \times b = b \times a$.

Example 1: $2 + 3 = 3 + 2$

- Each expression, $2 + 3$ and $3 + 2$, equals 5.
- The order of the addends, the numbers being added, does not matter.

Example 2: $4 \times 5 = 5 \times 4$

♦ Each expression, 4×5 and 5×4, equals 20.
♦ The order of the multiplicand, the number that is being multiplied, and the multiplier, the number that multiplies, does not matter.

The associative property states that the answer to an addition or multiplication problem will be the same regardless of how the numbers are grouped:

For all real numbers a, b, and c, $a + (b + c) = (a + b) + c$ and $a \times (b \times c) = (a \times b) \times c$.

The parentheses in the equations are grouping symbols. In determining the order of operations, operations within parentheses must be completed first.

Example 1: $4 + (3 + 2) = (4 + 3) + 2$

♦ On the left side of the equation, $(3 + 2)$ must be completed first because the operation is within parentheses. $(3 + 2) = 5$.
♦ Next, add 4 and 5, which equals 9.
♦ On the right side of the equation, $(4 + 3)$ must be completed first because the operation is within parentheses. $(4 + 3) = 7$.
♦ Next add 7 and 2, which equals 9.
♦ The expressions on each side of the equation equal 9.

Example 2: $5 \times (3 \times 2) = (5 \times 3) \times 2$

♦ On the left side of the equation, (3×2) must be completed first because the operation is within parentheses. $(3 \times 2) = 6$.
♦ Next, multiply 5 by 6, which equals 30.
♦ On the right side of the equation, (5×3) must be completed first because the operation is within parentheses. $(5 \times 3) = 15$.
♦ Next, multiply 15 by 2, which equals 30.
♦ The expressions on each side of the equation equal 30.

The number 1 has a special property called the multiplication property of 1. The multiplication property of 1 states that the product of any number and 1 equals the number:

For any real number a, $a \times 1 = a$ and $1 \times a = a$.
For example, $2 \times 1 = 2$ and $1 \times 2 = 2$.
(Note that 1 is also known as the multiplicative identity.)

Zero has two special properties: the addition property of zero and the multiplication property of zero.

The addition property of zero, also known as the identity property of addition, states that a number does not change in value when zero is added to it:

For any real number a, $a + 0 = a$ and $0 + a = a$.
For example, $2 + 0 = 2$ and $0 + 2 = 2$.
(Note that zero is called the additive identity.)

The multiplication property of zero states that the product of any number and zero equals zero:

For any real number a, $a \times 0 = 0$ and $0 \times a = 0$.
For example, $2 \times 0 = 0$ and $0 \times 2 = 0$.

Identify the property that is shown in each equation below.

1. $1 + 0 = 1$

2. $4 \times 5 \times 10 \times 0 = 0$

3. $(7 + 9) + 1 = 7 + (9 + 1)$

4. $45 \times (2 \times 3) = (45 \times 2) \times 3$

5. $25 \times 2 \times 3 \times 1 = 2 \times 25 \times 3 \times 1$

6. $19 + 35 = 35 + 19$

Complete each problem using an associative or commutative property of addition or multiplication. Write the name of the property you used.

7. Show that $100 + 35 = 35 + 100$.

8. Show that $4 \times 7 = 7 \times 4$.

9. Show that $(12 + 15) + 4 = 12 + (15 + 4)$.

10. Show that $(8 \times 3) \times 2 = 8 \times (3 \times 2)$.

11. Show that $(25 + 5) + 8 = 25 + (5 + 8)$.

12. Show that $5 \times (20 \times 7) = (5 \times 20) \times 7$.

13. In problem 11, which grouping makes the computation easier? Why?

14. In problem 12, which grouping makes computation easier? Why?

Operations with rational numbers

Adding integers with like signs

Integers are the set of natural numbers, their opposites, and zero. Addition of integers requires an understanding of basic addition and subtraction, as well as an understanding of absolute value.

A number line is often used to model addition of integers. For example, 3 + 2 can be modeled by starting at 3 and moving 2 units to the right, because a positive number is being added to 3. The sum is 5. (See Figure 2-1.)

Figure 2-1

To model −3 + (−2), start at −3 and move 2 units to the left, because a negative number is being added to −3. The sum is −5. (See Figure 2-2.)

Figure 2-2

To add two positive integers, simply add.

Example 1: 3 + 2

♦ Both numbers are positive. (Note that if a number has no sign, it is assumed to be positive.)
♦ The sum, of course, is 5.

To add two negative integers, add the absolute values of the integers and include the negative sign in your answer. The absolute value of a number is the number's distance from zero on a number line.

Example 2: $-3 + (-2)$

♦ Both numbers are negative.
♦ Add the absolute values of the numbers. $|-3| = 3$ and $|-2| = 2$. Add 3 and 2, which equals 5. The symbol, $|\ |$, represents the absolute value of a number.
♦ Because both integers are negative, their sum is a negative number. Place a negative sign next to the answer, 5, to arrive at the correct sum, −5.

Solve each addition problem below. Then write the letter of the problem in the space above its answer at the end of the exercise to complete the sentence. Some answers will be used more than once. Some answers will not be used.

G. 5 + 20

I. −7 + (−8)

R. −12 + (−5)

L. 3 + 8

F. −11 + (−8)

E. 13 + 13

C. −22 + (−1)

J. −5 + (−4)

N. −25 + (−11)

K. 32 + 54

O. −9 + (−9)

D. 15 + 32

A. −17 + (−10)

T. −1 + (−15)

P. −41 + (−27)

M. 54 + 16

H. −14 + (−27)

B. −61 + (−23)

Before computers, accountants kept records of clients' finances by hand, using two different colors of pens, red and black. They used the term

___ ___   ___ ___ ___   ___ ___ ___
−15 −36   −16 −41 26   −17 26 47

when clients were in debt and

___ ___   ___ ___ ___   ___ ___ ___ ___ ___
−15 −36   −16 −41 26   −84 11 −27 −23 86

when clients had more money than they had spent. These terms are still used today.

Complete each addition problem below.

1. 7 + 2

2. −3 + (−4)

3. 10 + 5

4. −5 + (−6)

5. −12 + (−8)

6. 31 + 54

7. −15 + (−21)

8. −62 + (−11)

9. −9 + (−36)

10. −24 + (−24)

11. 17 + 77

12. 28 + 82

13. −56 + (−18)

14. −9 + (−85)

15. −61 + (−92)

16. −29 + (−32)

Adding integers with unlike signs

When you add integers with unlike signs, you must use absolute value. Remember that the absolute value of a number is its distance from zero on the number line.

To model the addition of integers with unlike signs, use a number line. When adding integers with unlike signs, think of the positive and negative signs as directional signs. A positive sign tells you that you must move to the right. Moving to the right means an increase in value. A negative sign tells you that you must move left. Moving to the left means the value decreases.

Follow the steps below to model the addition of integers with unlike signs.

1. Begin with the first number in the expression.

2. If the second number in the expression is positive, move to the right the number of spaces you are adding. If the second number in the expression is negative, move to the left the number of spaces you are adding.

3. If there are more than two numbers to be added, continue this process for each number in the expression.

4. After moving the appropriate number of units, you will arrive at your answer.

For example, to model 4 + (−5) on a number line, begin at 4. Because the 5 you are adding is negative, move 5 units to the left. You will arrive at −1, which is the correct answer. (See Figure 2-3.)

Figure 2-3

To model −3 + 4 on the number line, begin at −3. Because 4 is positive, move 4 units to the right. You will arrive at 1, which is the correct answer. (See Figure 2-4.)

Figure 2-4

Although number lines can help you to visualize the addition process, they are not always practical for adding integers, especially large integers, with unlike signs. Instead you should use absolute value.

When integers have unlike signs, find the absolute value of each integer. Then subtract the smaller absolute value from the larger. Use the sign of the number with the larger absolute value in your answer.

Example 1: 4 + (−5)

- Find the absolute values of 4 and −5. $|4| = 4$ and $|-5| = 5$.
- Because 5 is larger than 4, subtract 4 from 5. 5 − 4 = 1. Since −5 has a larger absolute value than 4, the sign of 4 + (−5) is negative.
- The sum is −1.

Example 2: −3 + 4

- Find the absolute values of −3 and 4. $|-3| = 3$ and $|4| = 4$.
- Because 3 is less than 4, subtract 3 from 4. 4 − 3 = 1. Since 4 has a larger absolute value than −3, the sign of the answer is positive.
- The sum is 1.

Solve each addition problem below. Then write the letter of the problem in the space above its answer at the end of the exercise to find the answer to the question. Some answers will be used more than once. Some answers will not be used.

B. $8 + (-10)$
N. $-12 + 4$
A. $15 + (-9)$
I. $6 + (-2)$
M. $-18 + 8$
O. $-20 + 9$

U. $23 + (-20)$
L. $34 + (-41)$
F. $-45 + 12$
C. $-18 + 25$
S. $15 + (-45)$
D. $-62 + 21$

Which clouds often bring thunderstorms?

___ ___ ___ ___ ___ ___ ___ ___ ___ ___ ___ ___
7   3   −10   3   −7   −11   −8   4   −10   −2   3   −30

Complete each addition problem below.

1. $7 + (-3)$
2. $-15 + 11$
3. $21 + (-7)$
4. $10 + (-5)$
5. $-12 + 6$
6. $-11 + 17$
7. $-8 + 10$
8. $9 + (-3)$
9. $-17 + 19$
10. $-33 + 15$
11. $27 + (-4)$
12. $-51 + 23$
13. $-67 + 24$
14. $38 + (-47)$
15. $-10 + 10$
16. $-17 + 35$

Operations with rational numbers   **19**

Subtracting integers with like signs

As with the addition of integers, a number line can be used to model the subtraction of integers.

To model the subtraction of two positive numbers, you must move to the left on the number line because subtraction means taking away. When you take away a positive number from another positive number, the overall value decreases.

For example, to model 4 – 6, begin at 4 and move 6 units to the left. You will arrive at –2. (See Figure 2-5.)

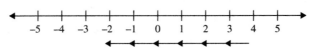

Figure 2-5

To use a number line to model the subtraction of two negative integers, the process is slightly different. When you subtract a negative number from a negative number, you move to the right, not the left. This is because you are taking away a negative, which increases the overall value.

For example, to model –3 – (–2), begin at –3. Move to the right 2 units because you are subtracting –2. You will arrive at –1. (See Figure 2-6.)

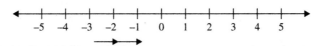

Figure 2-6

The best method for subtracting integers that have the same sign is to use the definition of subtraction. Stated algebraically, $a - b = a + (-b)$. To subtract integers that have the same sign, follow the steps below.

1. Leave the sign of the first number in the expression as is.

2. Change the subtraction sign to addition.

3. Change the sign of the second number in the expression to its opposite to rewrite the expression.

4. Follow the rules for adding integers with unlike signs.

   Example 1: 4 – 6

- The first number, 4, remains as is.
- Change the subtraction sign to addition.
- Change 6 to its opposite, –6. The new expression is 4 + (–6).
- Use the procedure for adding integers with unlike signs. Find the absolute values of 4 and –6. Because 4 is less than 6, subtract 4 from 6. The difference is 2. Because the absolute value of –6 is greater than the absolute value of 4, the answer is negative.
- The correct answer is –2.

   Example 2: –3 – (–2)

- The first number, –3, remains as is.
- Change the subtraction sign to addition.

- Change −2 to its opposite, 2. The new expression is −3 + 2.
- Use the procedure for adding integers with unlike signs. Find the absolute values of −3 and 2. Subtract 2 from 3. The difference is 1. Because the absolute value of −3 is greater than the absolute value of 2, the answer is negative.
- The correct answer is −1.

EXERCISE 2·5

Solve each subtraction problem below. Then write the letter of the problem in the space above its answer at the end of the exercise to complete the sentence. One answer will be used twice. Some answers will not be used.

L. −13 − (−4)

M. 21 − 13

A. 12 − 15

K. −17 − (−32)

I. −4 − (−8)

J. 45 − 51

U. 15 − 8

T. 12 − 9

H. −10 − (−19)

F. −19 − (−19)

R. −14 − (−4)

B. 37 − 51

Standing over 828 meters (2,716.5 feet) high, the

___ ___ ___ ___   ___ ___ ___ ___ ___ ___ ___
−14   7   −10   −6   15   9   −3   −9   4   0   −3

is the tallest building in the world.

EXERCISE 2·6

Complete each subtraction problem below.

1. 5 − 4

2. 2 − 3

3. −4 − (−7)

4. −3 − (−5)

5. 4 − 10

6. 7 − 12

7. −11 − (−9)

8. 8 − 6

9. 12 − 20

10. −16 − (−4)

11. −20 − (−10)

12. 36 − 12

13. −45 − (−51)

14. −71 − (−80)

15. 95 − 100

16. −63 − (−79)

Subtracting integers with unlike signs

To subtract integers with unlike signs, you must rewrite the problem using the definition of subtraction, $a − b = a + (−b)$, and then follow the rules for adding integers with like signs.

A number line is useful for modeling the subtraction of integers with unlike signs.

To model 3 − (−2), start at 3. Move 2 units to the right because you are subtracting a negative number. You will arrive at 5, which is the correct answer. (See Figure 2-7.)

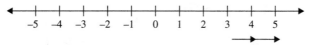

Figure 2-7

To model −1 − 3, start at −1. Move 3 units to the left because you are subtracting a positive number. You will arrive at −4, which is the correct answer. (See Figure 2-8.)

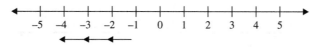

Figure 2-8

To subtract integers, use the definition of subtraction to rewrite the problem.

1. Leave the first number in the expression as is.

2. Change the subtraction sign to addition.

3. Change the sign of the second number to its opposite.

4. Follow the rules for adding integers with like signs.

Example 1: 3 − (−2)

- ◆ Leave 3 as is.
- ◆ Change the subtraction sign to addition.
- ◆ Change −2 to its opposite, 2. The new expression is 3 + 2.
- ◆ Add as you normally would to arrive at 5, which is the correct answer.

Example 2: –1 – 3

- ◆ Leave –1 as is.
- ◆ Change the subtraction sign to addition.
- ◆ Change 3 to –3. The new expression is –1 + (–3).
- ◆ Follow the steps for adding integers with like signs.
- ◆ The sum is –4.

EXERCISE 2·7

Solve each subtraction problem below. Then write the letter of the problem in the space above its answer at the end of the exercise to answer the question. Some answers will be used more than once. Some answers will not be used.

B. 7 – (–3)

U. –3 – 6

N. 9 – (–5)

D. –10 – 6

I. 8 – (–8)

G. –12 – 10

C. –16 – 7

O. 21 – (–8)

T. 34 – (–10)

M. –45 – 12

Q. –15 – 24

A. 17 – (–13)

S. –61 – 15

L. –52 – 21

What are the three states of matter on Earth?

__ __ __ __ __ __ ,   __ __ __ __ __ ,
−73 16 −39 −9 16 −16   −76 29 −73 16 −16

__ __ __
−22 30 −76

Complete each subtraction problem below.

1. $5 - (-3)$

2. $-4 - 6$

3. $-10 - 7$

4. $-8 - 12$

5. $15 - (-12)$

6. $21 - (-10)$

7. $-7 - 15$

8. $-25 - 30$

9. $32 - (-40)$

10. $63 - (-24)$

11. $-59 - 70$

12. $11 - (-11)$

13. $75 - (-25)$

14. $-68 - 21$

15. $42 - (-15)$

16. $-83 - 31$

Multiplying integers

In pre-algebra and other higher-level math classes, you will see multiplication shown in a variety of ways. The sign ×, a raised dot ·, and parentheses are all used to show multiplication. Each of the following expressions, 5×4, $5 \cdot 4$, and $(5)(4)$, means that you must multiply 5 and 4. The product (the answer to the multiplication problem) is 20.

When multiplying integers, you must find the products of their absolute values. Keep in mind the following rules to find the correct sign of the product.

- The product of two positive integers is a positive integer.
- The product of a positive integer and a negative integer (or the product of a negative integer and a positive integer) is a negative integer.
- The product of two negative integers is a positive integer.
- The product of any integer and zero is zero.

    Example 1: 5×4

- Because 5 and 4 are both positive, multiply as you normally would.
- The product is positive: 20.

Example 2: (2)(–3)

- ♦ Multiply the absolute values of the integers: $2 \times 3 = 6$.
- ♦ Because you are multiplying a positive 2 by a negative 3, the answer is negative.
- ♦ The product is –6.

Example 3: –7(–2)

- ♦ Multiply the absolute values of the integers: $7 \times 2 = 14$.
- ♦ Because both factors are negative, the answer is positive.
- ♦ The product is 14.

EXERCISE
2·9

Complete each multiplication problem below.

1. -7×7

2. $5 \times (-4)$

3. $(6)(-3)$

4. $(-10)(-4)$

5. 12×5

6. -3×11

7. $(-15)(-4)$

8. $(24)(-3)$

9. $17 \times (-1)$

10. $-4 \times (-4)$

11. 33×5

12. $42(-6)$

13. $-51 \times (-2)$

14. $-8 \times (-8)$

15. $(9)(-7)$

16. $-6(-4)$

Dividing integers

As with multiplication, division can also be shown in different ways. Both the division sign ÷, and the fraction bar show division. For example, $20 \div 5$ and $\dfrac{20}{5}$ can both be used to express 20 divided by 5. In both cases, the quotient, or answer to the division problem, is 4.

When dividing integers, you must find the quotient of their absolute values. Keep in mind the following rules to find the correct sign of the quotient.

- When the divisor (the number you divide by) and dividend (the number you divide) are both positive, the quotient is a positive number.
- When the divisor or dividend is positive, and the other is negative, the quotient is a negative number.
- When the divisor and dividend are both negative, the quotient is a positive number.
- When zero is divided by any integer, the quotient is zero.
- You cannot divide by zero. The quotient is undefined.

   Example 1: $30 \div 6$

- Both 30 and 6 are positive.
- Divide 30 by 6.
- The quotient is 5.

   Example 2: $-42 \div 7$

- 42 is negative but 7 is positive.
- Divide the absolute value of −42 by the absolute value of 7: $42 \div 7 = 6$.
- Because one of the terms is positive and the other is negative, the quotient is negative: −6.

   Example 3: $\dfrac{-20}{-2}$

- Divide the absolute value of −20 by the absolute value of −2: $20 \div 2 = 10$.
- Because both integers are negative, the quotient is positive, 10.

   Example 4: $\dfrac{0}{3}$

- Zero divided by any number is zero. The quotient is 0.

   Example 5: $\dfrac{3}{0}$

- It is impossible to divide by zero.
- The quotient is undefined.

Complete each division problem below.

1. $25 \div 5$

2. $-30 \div 6$

3. $\dfrac{-42}{-7}$

4. $0 \div 2$

5. $\dfrac{56}{8}$

6. $64 \div (-8)$

7. $-36 \div 4$

8. $-70 \div (-10)$

9. $\dfrac{81}{-9}$

10. $\dfrac{16}{0}$

11. $-60 \div (-5)$

12. $\dfrac{24}{-6}$

13. $39 \div (-3)$

14. $104 \div 2$

15. $\dfrac{132}{-12}$

16. $\dfrac{-81}{-3}$

Adding rational numbers with like signs

A rational number is defined as a number that can be expressed as the quotient of two integers, a fraction $\frac{a}{b}$, where a and b are integers and $b \neq 0$. Rational numbers include the sets of integers, whole numbers, and natural numbers. They also include fractions and terminating and repeating decimals.

The process for adding rational numbers with like signs is similar to the methods for adding integers with like signs. If both rational numbers are positive, simply add. If both rational numbers are negative, find the absolute value of each number and add the absolute values. The sign of the answer is negative.

Example 1: $0.25 + 0.8$
Example 2: $-0.25 + (-0.80)$

In Example 1, both rational numbers are positive. Therefore, the sum is positive, 1.05.

In Example 2, -0.25 and -0.8 are both negative numbers. Because they have the same sign, find the absolute value of each number. The absolute value of -0.25 is 0.25, and the absolute value of -0.8 is 0.8. Add $0.25 + 0.8$, which equals 1.05. Because both rational numbers are negative, the sum is -1.05.

Example 3: $\frac{1}{4} + \frac{4}{5}$

Example 4: $-\frac{1}{4} + \left(-\frac{4}{5}\right)$

In these examples, the fractions have like signs. To add fractions, remember to find the common denominator, write equivalent fractions, add the fractions, and simplify the sum, if possible.

In Example 3, the least common denominator of 4 and 5 is 20. To write equivalent fractions using 20 as the denominator, $\frac{1}{4}$ is expressed as $\frac{5}{20}$ and $\frac{4}{5}$ is expressed as $\frac{16}{20}$. Add $\frac{5}{20} + \frac{16}{20}$ which equals $\frac{21}{20}$. Because $\frac{21}{20}$ is an improper fraction (the numerator is greater than the denominator), rewrite it as a mixed number. Divide 21 by 20 to find 1 with $\frac{1}{20}$ left over. The sum is $1\frac{1}{20}$.

In Example 4, the process for adding fractions is the same. But because both fractions are negative, you must first find the absolute value of each fraction and then add. The absolute value of $-\frac{1}{4}$ is $\frac{1}{4}$ and the absolute value of $-\frac{4}{5}$ is $\frac{4}{5}$. Find the least common denominator, write equivalent fractions, add, and simplify the answer. Then place a negative sign in the sum because both fractions are negative. The correct sum is $-1\frac{1}{20}$.

Solve each addition problem below. Then write the letter of the problem in the space above its answer at the end of the exercise to complete the sentence. Some answers will be used more than once. Some answers will not be used.

S. $-\dfrac{3}{4} + \left(-\dfrac{7}{9}\right)$

I. $0.35 + 0.14$

H. $-0.2 + (-0.78)$

R. $-4.5 + (-1.3)$

C. $\dfrac{7}{8} + \dfrac{1}{2}$

O. $1.2 + 3.8$

A. $-\dfrac{4}{5} + \left(-\dfrac{1}{6}\right)$

B. $-\dfrac{4}{5} + (-0.7)$

L. $1\dfrac{2}{3} + \dfrac{4}{9}$

T. $-2\dfrac{2}{5} + \left(-3\dfrac{1}{6}\right)$

N. $-2.1 + (-0.4)$

M. $1.75 + 3\dfrac{6}{7}$

K. $7.05 + 6.4$

U. $-1\dfrac{3}{5} + \left(-1\dfrac{1}{2}\right)$

The United States bought Alaska from

___ ___ ___ ___ ___ ___

-5.8 $-3\dfrac{1}{10}$ $-1\dfrac{19}{36}$ $-1\dfrac{19}{36}$ 0.49 $-\dfrac{29}{30}$

in 1867 for \$7.2 ___ ___ ___ ___ ___ ___ ___ .

$5\dfrac{17}{28}$ 0.49 $2\dfrac{1}{9}$ $2\dfrac{1}{9}$ 0.49 5 -2.5

Complete each addition problem below.

1. $-0.4 + (-0.35)$

2. $\dfrac{3}{5} + \dfrac{2}{7}$

3. $-\dfrac{1}{8} + \left(-\dfrac{3}{4}\right)$

4. $-0.92 + (-0.32)$

5. $-\dfrac{5}{7} + \left(-\dfrac{2}{5}\right)$

6. $1.82 + 0.54$

7. $-2.5 + (-1.3)$

8. $-\dfrac{6}{7} + \left(-1\dfrac{2}{3}\right)$

9. $2\dfrac{1}{4} + 2\dfrac{5}{6}$

10. $-1.9 + (-2.4)$

11. $-3\dfrac{4}{5} + \left(-\dfrac{7}{10}\right)$

12. $8.1 + 0.45$

13. $-5.2 + (-0.6)$

14. $-4\dfrac{1}{2} + \left(-1\dfrac{3}{4}\right)$

15. $-0.8 + \left(-\dfrac{1}{3}\right)$

16. $-2\dfrac{1}{3} + (-0.75)$

Adding rational numbers with unlike signs

The steps for adding rational numbers with unlike signs are similar to the steps for adding integers with unlike signs. First find the absolute value of each rational number in the expression. Then subtract the smaller absolute value from the larger absolute value. Place the sign of the number with the larger absolute value in your answer.

Example 1: $-1.2 + 0.7$

◆ Find the absolute value of each number.
◆ The absolute value of -1.2 is 1.2. The absolute value of 0.7 is 0.7. Rewrite the problem by lining up the decimal points to subtract the smaller absolute value from the larger.

$$\begin{array}{r} 1.2 \\ -\,\underline{0.7} \end{array}$$

◆ Subtract as you normally would to find 0.5.
◆ Next, consider the absolute values.
◆ Since -1.2 has a larger absolute value than 0.7, the answer is negative.
◆ The sum is -0.5.

Example 2: $\dfrac{5}{6} + \left(-\dfrac{1}{2}\right)$

◆ Find the absolute value of each number. The absolute value of $\dfrac{5}{6}$ is $\dfrac{5}{6}$. The absolute value of $-\dfrac{1}{2}$ is $\dfrac{1}{2}$.
◆ Subtract $\dfrac{1}{2}$ from $\dfrac{5}{6}$ because $\dfrac{1}{2}$ is less than $\dfrac{5}{6}$. Find the least common denominator, write an equivalent fraction, and rewrite the problem as $\dfrac{5}{6} - \dfrac{3}{6}$.
◆ Subtract the fractions to find $\dfrac{2}{6}$, which can be simplified as $\dfrac{1}{3}$. Because the absolute value of $\dfrac{5}{6}$ is larger than the absolute value of $-\dfrac{1}{2}$, the answer is positive.
◆ The sum is $\dfrac{1}{3}$.

Solve each addition problem below. Then write the letter of the problem in the space above its answer at the end of the exercise to complete the sentence. Some answers will be used more than once. Some answers will not be used.

N. $-0.9 + 0.7$

E. $-2\dfrac{3}{4} + 3\dfrac{3}{7}$

T. $\dfrac{1}{2} + \left(-\dfrac{1}{8}\right)$

L. $8.23 + (-5.78)$

I. $-\dfrac{3}{5} + \dfrac{7}{15}$

D. $4\dfrac{1}{2} + (-0.4)$

C. $0.18 + (-0.75)$

Y. $-3.75 + \dfrac{3}{8}$

W. $-1.4 + 3.6$

R. $-2.2 + 0.8$

M. $-2\dfrac{5}{6} + 1.25$

B. $1\dfrac{2}{3} + \left(-\dfrac{4}{5}\right)$

The

$\underline{}$ $\underline{}$ $\underline{}$ $\underline{}$ $\underline{}$ $\underline{}$ $\underline{}$ $\underline{}$ $\underline{}$ $\underline{}$ $\underline{}$

2.45 $\quad -\dfrac{2}{15}$ $\quad \dfrac{13}{15}$ $\quad \dfrac{19}{28}$ $\quad -1.4$ $\quad \dfrac{3}{8}$ $\quad -3.375$ $\qquad \dfrac{13}{15}$ $\quad \dfrac{19}{28}$ $\quad$ 2.45 $\quad$ 2.45

is engraved with the historic words, "Proclaim Liberty throughout all the Land unto all the inhabitants thereof."

Solve each addition problem below.

1. $-0.9 + 0.4$

2. $-\dfrac{1}{2} + \dfrac{6}{7}$

3. $1.5 + (-1.2)$

4. $6.1 + (-7.4)$

5. $-\dfrac{2}{3} + \dfrac{4}{5}$

6. $\dfrac{9}{10} + \left(-\dfrac{13}{15}\right)$

7. $-1.34 + 2$

8. $0.81 + (-0.32)$

9. $\dfrac{11}{12} + \left(-\dfrac{1}{6}\right)$

10. $1\dfrac{2}{5} + \left(-\dfrac{7}{10}\right)$

11. $-4.5 + 0.67$

12. $-2.55 + 3.12$

13. $\dfrac{8}{11} + \left(-2\dfrac{1}{2}\right)$

14. $-3\dfrac{1}{2} + 0.75$

15. $9.1 + \left(-\dfrac{3}{10}\right)$

16. $-2.5 + \left(3\dfrac{4}{5}\right)$

Subtracting rational numbers with like or unlike signs

Subtracting rational numbers is very similar to subtracting integers. To subtract rational numbers with like or unlike signs, follow the steps below.

1. Leave the first number in the expression as is.

2. Change the subtraction sign to addition.

3. Change the sign of the second number to its opposite.

4. Follow the rules for adding rational numbers.

   Example 1: $-0.75 - (-0.8)$

- Leave -0.75 as is.
- Change the subtraction sign to addition. Change -0.8 to its opposite, 0.8.
- The new expression is $-0.75 + 0.8$.
- Add as you would add rational numbers with unlike signs.
- The answer is 0.05.

   Example 2: $1\frac{2}{3} - \left(-\frac{5}{6}\right)$

- Express the mixed number as an improper fraction. $1\frac{2}{3} = \frac{5}{3}$.

- Find the least common denominator and write an equivalent fraction for $\frac{5}{3}$: $\frac{5}{3} = \frac{10}{6}$.

- Rewrite the problem as $\frac{10}{6} - \left(-\frac{5}{6}\right)$.

- Change the subtraction sign to addition. Change $-\frac{5}{6}$ to its opposite, $\frac{5}{6}$.

- The new expression is $\frac{10}{6} + \frac{5}{6}$.

- Add the fractions.

- The answer is $\frac{15}{6} = 2\frac{1}{2}$.

Solve each addition problem below. Then write the letter of the problem in the space above its answer at the end of the exercise to complete the sentence. Some answers will be used more than once. Some answers will not be used.

A. $\dfrac{2}{5} - \dfrac{7}{10}$

C. $-5\dfrac{1}{6} - \left(-2\dfrac{1}{3}\right)$

I. $-2\dfrac{1}{3} - \dfrac{5}{6}$

F. $-1.57 - 0.3$

E. $-0.42 - (-0.78)$

L. $13 - \left(-\dfrac{8}{9}\right)$

D. $2.45 - 5.6$

P. $-12.3 - \dfrac{7}{8}$

N. $-\dfrac{9}{10} - \left(-\dfrac{1}{4}\right)$

M. $\dfrac{2}{7} - (-1.5)$

The average

___ ___ ___ ___   ___ ___ ___ ___ ___ ___

$13\dfrac{8}{9}$ 0.36 $-\dfrac{3}{10}$ -3.15 $-13\dfrac{7}{40}$ 0.36 $-\dfrac{13}{20}$ $-2\dfrac{5}{6}$ $-3\dfrac{1}{6}$ $13\dfrac{8}{9}$

can draw a line that is almost 35 miles long or write about 50,000 words in English!

Complete each subtraction problem below.

1. $\dfrac{3}{4} - \left(-\dfrac{7}{8}\right)$

2. $-\dfrac{4}{5} - \left(-\dfrac{4}{15}\right)$

3. $-0.55 - 0.32$

4. $0.9 - (-0.43)$

5. $-2.5 - (-0.64)$

6. $1\dfrac{1}{2} - 3\dfrac{3}{4}$

7. $-\dfrac{6}{7} - \left(-\dfrac{1}{6}\right)$

8. $3.4 - 8.56$

9. $-\dfrac{2}{7} - \dfrac{7}{8}$

10. $\dfrac{19}{20} - 3\dfrac{2}{5}$

11. $-6.21 - (-6.21)$

12. $\dfrac{4}{5} - \dfrac{2}{9}$

13. $10.25 - (-14.2)$

14. $3\dfrac{5}{9} - (-8.9)$

15. $-12.1 - \dfrac{1}{5}$

16. $1.8 - 4\dfrac{1}{2}$

Multiplying rational numbers

The rules for multiplying rational numbers are the same as the rules for multiplying integers. Multiply the absolute values of the numbers. Keep in mind the following to find the correct sign.

♦ The product of two positive rational numbers is a positive rational number.
♦ The product of a positive rational number and a negative rational number is a negative rational number.
♦ The product of two negative rational numbers is a positive rational number.
♦ The product of any rational number and zero is zero.

When multiplying rational numbers, you must also remember the rules for multiplying fractions and decimals. Use the examples below as a guide.

Example 1: $(-1.2)(-1.6)$

♦ Rewrite the problem vertically and multiply the absolute values as you would multiply whole numbers.

$$
\begin{array}{r}
1.2 \\
\times 1.6 \\
\hline
72 \\
+120 \\
\hline
1.92
\end{array}
$$

♦ To place the decimal point correctly in the product, count the number of digits to the right of the decimal points in your factors. (1.2 has one digit to the right of the decimal point. 1.6 also has one digit to the right of the decimal point. The product should have a total of two digits to the right of the decimal point.)
♦ Start at the right of the product and move to the left the total number of decimal places that you counted in the factors. Place the decimal point there.
♦ Because two negative numbers were multiplied, the product is positive.
♦ The product is 1.92.

Example 2: $-\dfrac{2}{3} \times \dfrac{4}{5}$

♦ Multiply the absolute values of the fractions. $\dfrac{2}{3} \times \dfrac{4}{5} = \dfrac{8}{15}$.

♦ Because $-\dfrac{2}{3}$ is negative and $\dfrac{4}{5}$ is positive, the product is negative.

♦ The product is $-\dfrac{8}{15}$.

Complete each multiplication problem below.

1. $-\dfrac{2}{3} \times \dfrac{7}{8}$

2. $(-0.3)(-0.9)$

3. $\dfrac{1}{9} \times \left(-\dfrac{3}{5}\right)$

4. $(-1.3)(2.4)$

5. $1\dfrac{2}{3} \times \dfrac{4}{7}$

6. $1.5(-0.8)$

7. $\left(-\dfrac{1}{6}\right)\left(-\dfrac{1}{6}\right)$

8. $-3.6(-2.3)$

9. $-2\dfrac{1}{2} \times 2\dfrac{3}{4}$

10. $(1.9)(-2.78)$

11. $\left(-\dfrac{9}{10}\right)\left(-\dfrac{3}{4}\right)$

12. $5\dfrac{3}{4} \times 3$

13. $5.7(-0.45)$

14. $(-0.6)(-0.2)$

15. $-\dfrac{4}{9} \times \dfrac{12}{13}$

16. $-3(-0.5)$

Dividing rational numbers

The rules for dividing rational numbers are the same as the rules for dividing integers. You must divide the absolute values of the numbers. Keep in mind the following to place the correct sign in the quotient.

- When the divisor and dividend are both positive rational numbers, the quotient is a positive rational number.
- When the divisor or dividend is a positive rational number and the other is a negative rational number, the quotient is a negative rational number.
- When the divisor and dividend are both negative rational numbers, the quotient is a positive rational number.
- When zero is divided by a rational number, the quotient is zero.
- You cannot divide by zero. The quotient is undefined.

    Example 1: $0.9 \div (-0.3)$

- Find the absolute values of the numbers and rewrite the problem as $0.3\overline{)0.9}$.
- Move each decimal point one place to the right in the divisor and dividend so that you are dividing by an integer. (Moving the decimal point one place to the right is the same as multiplying the number by 10.)
- Rewrite the problem as $3\overline{)9}$.
- Divide as you normally would. The quotient is 3. Because you are dividing a positive number by a negative number, your answer is negative.
- The quotient is -3.

    Example 2: $-\dfrac{1}{2} \div \left(-\dfrac{3}{4}\right)$

- Find the absolute values of the numbers and rewrite the problem as $\dfrac{1}{2} \div \dfrac{3}{4}$.

- Find the reciprocal of the second fraction by rewriting the numerator as the denominator and the denominator as the numerator. The reciprocal of $\dfrac{3}{4}$ is $\dfrac{4}{3}$.

- Change the division sign to multiplication and rewrite the problem as $\dfrac{1}{2} \times \left(\dfrac{4}{3}\right)$.

- The product is $\dfrac{4}{6}$, which can be simplified as $\dfrac{2}{3}$.

- Because you multiplied two negative numbers, the answer is positive.

- The quotient is $\dfrac{2}{3}$.

Complete each division problem below.

1. $-0.8 \div (-0.2)$

2. $\dfrac{2}{5} \div \left(-\dfrac{3}{4}\right)$

3. $\dfrac{1.2}{3.6}$

4. $-\dfrac{4}{5} \div \left(-\dfrac{7}{8}\right)$

5. $-0.15 \div 0.5$

6. $\dfrac{3}{8} \div \dfrac{1}{2}$

7. $-2.4 \div (-0.6)$

8. $\dfrac{-1}{0.5}$

9. $1\dfrac{2}{3} \div \left(-\dfrac{2}{9}\right)$

10. $-3 \div \dfrac{1}{3}$

11. $-3.6 \div (-2)$

12. $12 \div (-0.4)$

13. $2\dfrac{6}{7} \div 1\dfrac{3}{4}$

14. $\dfrac{-4.5}{-0.9}$

15. $\dfrac{9}{10} \div (-0.2)$

16. $-1.8 \div \left(-\dfrac{4}{5}\right)$

Using the order of operations

The order of operations serves as a set of rules for arithmetic. The arithmetic *operations* referred to include addition, subtraction, multiplication, and division. The established *order* of these operations lays out the steps in which the operations should be completed. Following the order of operations ensures that problems are solved in the same order and result in the same answers.

Following are the steps for using the order of operations.

1. Operations within grouping symbols must be performed first. (Parentheses and the fraction bar are two types of grouping symbols.) When completing the operations within grouping symbols, follow the other steps for using the order of operations.

2. Multiply and divide in order from left to right. (If division appears before multiplication, divide first, then multiply.)

3. Add and subtract in order from left to right. (If subtraction appears before addition in the problem, subtract first, then add.)

It is helpful to rewrite the problem after you complete each operation. This will help you avoid careless mistakes.

Example 1: $5 + 2 \times 7$

- Multiplication must be performed before addition. Multiply 2 and 7. The product is 14.
- Rewrite the problem as $5 + 14$.
- Add 5 and 14.
- The answer is 19.

Example 2: $3 \div 2(5 - 7)$

- The expression within the grouping symbols must be simplified first. Subtract 7 from 5. The result is –2.
- Rewrite the problem as $3 \div 2 \times (-2)$.

- Multiply and divide in order from left to right. Since the division appears before the multiplication, divide 3 by 2. The quotient is $1\frac{1}{2}$.
- Rewrite the problem as $1\frac{1}{2} \times (-2)$. Express $1\frac{1}{2}$ as $\frac{3}{2}$ and multiply by –2.
- The answer is –3.

Example 3: $\dfrac{2 + 4(3)}{7} \times 5$

- Because the fraction bar is a grouping symbol, the fraction must be simplified first. Simplify the numerator, following the order of operations. Multiply 4 by 3, then add 2. The numerator is equal to 14. Divide the numerator by 7 and simplify the fraction as 2.
- Rewrite the problem as 2×5.
- The answer is 10.

Solve each problem below. Then write the letter of the problem in the space above its answer at the end of the exercise to complete the sentence. Some answers will be used more than once. One answer will not be used.

A. $14 - 10 \times 2 - 6$

D. $-3(4 - 8)$

E. $-3 - 6 + 7 - 4$

I. $\dfrac{2 \times 4}{12} \times 6$

S. $-12 \times 2 \div 3$

P. $-2(3 - 6) + 4$

R. $-5 - 4 \times 6$

L. $3 + 2 \times (-9)$

F. $3 + 4(8 - 2)$

O. $\dfrac{10}{7 + 3} - 4 \cdot 8$

N. $-12 \div 3 \times 6$

T. $3 + 8 - 4(-5)$

The first European mathematician to use the horizontal fraction bar was

___	___	___	___	___	___	___	___		___	___
−15	−6	−31	−24	−12	−29	12	−31		−31	27

___	___	___	___.
10	4	−8	−12

He is also known as Fibonacci.

Complete each problem below, following the order of operations.

1. $4 - 3 \times 6$

2. $2 + 6(3 - 10)$

3. $3 + (-4) - 6$

4. $4 - 8 \cdot 3 - 1$

5. $-10 - 4 \times 2 - 6$

6. $2 - 3 - 4$

7. $-3(-5) - 4 \cdot 8$

8. $(15 - 12)(2)$

9. $3(-6 - 4)8$

10. $9 \cdot 3 - 7$

11. $14 - 4(5 - 7)$

12. $9(3 - 7)$

13. $3(-4) - 6$

14. $(15 - 5) \div 2$

15. $\dfrac{3 \cdot 2 + 2}{4} - 8$

16. $\left(\dfrac{7 - 1}{6}\right) + (-6)$

Using absolute value

The absolute value of a number is defined as the distance that a number is from zero on a number line. Absolute value can be used to simplify expressions or solve equations.

The absolute value of 4, expressed as $|4|$, is 4 because the distance between 4 and zero is 4 units. The absolute value of -4, expressed as $|-4|$, is also 4. -4 is 4 units from 0. Absolute value asks: "how far?" or "what is the distance?" Since a distance is positive, the absolute value of a number is positive. Zero is the only exception to this rule. The absolute value of zero is zero.

Absolute value symbols are a type of grouping symbol. (Other grouping symbols include parentheses and the fraction bar.) When simplifying expressions, the operations within the absolute value symbols must be done first, according to the order of operations.

Example 1: $-|-7|$

- Simplify $|-7|$, which equals 7.
- The negative sign before the absolute value symbol is read as "the opposite of." Find the opposite of 7, which is -7.

Example 2: $|8 + (-9)|$

- Simplify the expression within the absolute value symbol, $8 + (-9)$ first. $8 + (-9) = -1$.
- Simplify $|-1|$, which equals 1.

Example 3: $|4 - 6 \times 2| + 6$

- Simplify the expression within the absolute value symbol, $4 - 6 \times 2$, first following the order of operations. Multiply 6 by 2, which equals 12, then subtract the product from 4. $4 - 12 = -8$.
- Simplify $|-8|$, which equals 8.
- Add 6.
- The answer is 14.

Simplify each expression below.

1. $|3|$

2. $|5 - (-1)| + 7$

3. $|-8 \cdot 2|$

4. $-4|-9 - 4|$

5. $5|-10|$

6. $-|13 + (-15)| + 12$

7. $-|17 - 5|$

8. $-2|0 - (-19)|$

9. $9|0|$

10. $|-5 + 5|$

11. $-|6|$

12. $|-5| + |5|$

13. $-|-15|$

14. $|10 \div 5| - 5$

15. $|-10 + (-2)|$

16. $|-6 \times (-6)|$

Simplifying exponents

An exponent, sometimes called a power, is an abbreviated form of multiplication. It is the number that appears above and to the right of a number called the base. The exponent represents the number of times the base is used as a factor. For example, the expression $3 \times 3 \times 3 \times 3$ can be expressed as 3^4. The exponent, 4, represents the number of times 3 is multiplied by itself. 3^4 is read "3 to the fourth power" and equals 81.

Two powers have special names. x^2 is read as "x to the second power," "x squared," or the "square of x." x^3 is read as "x to the third power," "x cubed," or the "cube of x." In both cases, x is a real number.

To simply exponents, multiply the base by itself the number of times indicated by the exponent.

Example 1: 2^4

- 2 is the base and 4 is the exponent.
- Rewrite this expression as $2 \times 2 \times 2 \times 2$ and multiply.
- The product is 16.

Example 2: $(-3)^6$

- −3 is the base and 6 is the exponent.
- Rewrite this expression as $-3 \times (-3) \times (-3) \times (-3) \times (-3) \times (-3)$.
- The product is 729.

Example 3: -3^6

- 3 is the base and 6 is the exponent. The negative symbol in front of this expression means the opposite of 3^6.
- Rewrite this expression as $-(3 \times 3 \times 3 \times 3 \times 3 \times 3)$.
- The product is −729.

Exponents can be positive numbers, negative numbers, or zero. By definition, any base except zero raised to the zero power is equal to 1. If x is a nonzero number, $x^0 = 1$. For example, 1^0, 10^0, and $(-5)^0$ all equal 1. Note that 0^0 is undefined.

If the exponent of the base is a negative number, the expression can be rewritten so that the base is in the denominator of a fraction. If x represents any nonzero number and n represents any positive integer, x^{-n} is the reciprocal of x^n. x^{-n} can be expressed as $\dfrac{1}{x^n}$.

Example 1: 7^0

- Because 7 is raised to the zero power, the answer is 1.

Example 2: -4^0

- 4 raised to the zero power is equal to 1. The opposite of 1 is −1.
- The answer is −1.

Example 3: 2^{-3}

- This can be rewritten as $\dfrac{1}{2^3}$. $2^3 = 2 \times 2 \times 2 = 8$.
- The answer is $\dfrac{1}{8}$.

Example 4: 6^{-2}

- This can be rewritten as $\dfrac{1}{6^2}$. $6^2 = 6 \times 6 = 36$.
- The answer is $\dfrac{1}{36}$.

EXERCISE
2·22

Choose the correct answer to each problem provided. Then write the letter of the answer in the space above its problem number at the end of the exercise to complete the sentence.

1. 2^5

32	10	16
C	D	I

2. -1^0

−1	0	1
I	L	Z

3. 3^0

3	1	0
B	I	X

4. 5^{-3}

−125	$\dfrac{1}{125}$	−15
R	N	S

5. 4^{-4}

$\dfrac{1}{4}$	−16	$\dfrac{1}{256}$
N	G	O

6. 6^3

216	36	18
S	T	W

7. -5^2

−25	25	−10
L	F	Y

After oxygen,

___ ___ ___ ___ ___ ___ ___
 6   3   7   2   1   5   4

is the most abundant element on Earth, making up more than a quarter of the Earth's crust.

Simplify each expression below.

1. 2^3

2. 3^{-3}

3. 4^2

4. -4^{-2}

5. 6^{-4}

6. 2^6

7. 10^3

8. -8^0

9. -8^2

10. 20^2

11. 7^3

12. 11^{-2}

13. 9^0

14. -3^{-1}

15. -2^5

16. -2^{-7}

Finding the square roots of perfect squares

Many operations have an opposite or inverse. Subtraction is the opposite of addition. Division is the opposite of multiplication. Finding the square root of a number means finding a number that, when raised to the power of 2, will make the original number. It is the opposite of squaring a number.

The square root of a number x is shown by $\sqrt{x}$ or $x^{\frac{1}{2}}$. The $\sqrt{\ }$ is called the radical symbol. The number within the radical symbol is called the radicand. The square root of any perfect square is an integer. The first 10 perfect squares are 1, 4, 9, 16, 25, 36, 49, 64, 81, and 100. Each is a product of a number and itself.

To find the square root of a perfect square, think about which integer multiplied by itself is equal to the radicand. If the radicand is a perfect square, then the square root is an integer. Every perfect square has two square roots: a positive square root and a negative square root. The radical symbol refers to the positive square root, which is also called the principal square root.

Example 1: Find $\sqrt{25}$.

- 25 is a perfect square.
- Think what number times itself equals 25. $5 \times 5 = 25$ or $5^2 = 25$ and $-5 \times (-5) = 25$.
- $\sqrt{25}$ refers to the positive square root.
- $\sqrt{25} = 5$.

Example 2: Find $\sqrt{81}$.

- 81 is a perfect square.
- Think what number times itself equals 81. $9 \times 9 = 81$ or $9^2 = 81$ and $-9 \times (-9) = 81$.
- $\sqrt{81}$ refers to the positive square root.
- $\sqrt{81} = 9$.

EXERCISE
2·24

Find each square root. Your answers will reveal the roots of all the perfect squares from 1 to 256. It may be helpful to memorize these for ease with calculations.

1. $\sqrt{36}$
2. $\sqrt{169}$
3. $\sqrt{4}$
4. $\sqrt{144}$
5. $\sqrt{64}$
6. $\sqrt{49}$
7. $\sqrt{9}$
8. $\sqrt{196}$
9. $\sqrt{1}$
10. $\sqrt{121}$
11. $\sqrt{25}$
12. $\sqrt{81}$
13. $\sqrt{100}$
14. $\sqrt{225}$
15. $\sqrt{256}$
16. $\sqrt{16}$

The order of operations (including exponents)

PEMDAS or Please Excuse My Dear Aunt Sally is a useful acronym for remembering the order in which operations are to be performed. Below are the words represented by the acronym.

- P: Parentheses (and other grouping symbols, working from the innermost parentheses out)
- E: Exponents, including square roots
- M: Multiplication
- D: Division
- A: Addition
- S: Subtraction

The phrase "Please Excuse My Dear Aunt Sally" will help you remember the acronym, which will remind you of the order in which to simplify an expression. If there are expressions within parentheses, or any other grouping symbols, you must simplify them first. Then simplify any base with its exponent and represent the result as a number. Although multiplication appears before division in the acronym, multiplication and division are completed in order from left to right. If division occurs first in a problem, divide before multiplying. Remember that multiplication and division, or either one of them, must always be performed before addition and subtraction. Addition and subtraction are also completed in order from left to right. If subtraction appears before addition in the problem, subtract before adding.

When solving problems with several operations, it is helpful to rewrite the problem after you complete each operation. This will help you avoid careless mistakes.

Example 1: $2(3 + 4 \times 7)$

- Complete the operations within parentheses. Of the operations in the parentheses, multiplication comes before addition. Multiply 4×7. Rewrite the problem as $2(3 + 28)$. Still working within the parentheses, add 3 and 28, which equals 31.
- Rewrite the problem as $2(31)$.
- Multiply 2×31.
- The answer is 62.

Example 2: $3 - \left(\sqrt{25} \times 4\right) + 4 \div 2$

- Complete the operations in parentheses. Simplify $\sqrt{25}$, which equals 5. Rewrite the problem as $3 - (5 \times 4) + 4 \div 2$. Still working within the parentheses, multiply 5 by 4, which equals 20.
- Rewrite the problem as $3 - 20 + 4 \div 2$.
- Division comes before addition or subtraction. Divide 4 by 2, which equals 2.
- Rewrite the problem as $3 - 20 + 2$.
- Because the subtraction in this problem appears before the addition, subtract 20 from 3, which equals –17.
- Rewrite the problem as $-17 + 2$.
- The answer is –15.

Complete each problem using the order of operations. Then write the letter of the answer in the space above its problem number at the end of the exercise to complete the sentence. Some answers are used more than once. Some answers will not be used.

D. $3^3 - 4 \times 5 \div 2$

I. $(4 \times 3)^2 \div 2 \times 1^0$

T. $\dfrac{20}{4} \times 3 - (5 + 8)$

X. $25 \div 5 + (4 \times 9 - 50)$

B. $6 \div (-2) + \sqrt{49} \times 2^3$

O. $15 + \left|-2 \times (-3)\right| - 16 \div (-4)$

A. $24 + 3 \times 7 - (5 + (2 + 3))$

R. $3(2 + 5(1 + 2))$

N. $\left|-7\right| - (4^2 + 3 + 2) - 12 \div 2$

M. $72 - \sqrt{100} \times 2 \times 3 + 3^2$

The Statue of Liberty was presented to the people of the United States by the people of France in 1886 as a gift to honor the friendship between the countries. The statue is formed of copper sheets attached to an iron frame. Over time, the copper turned green, resulting in the statue's present appearance. The process that causes copper to turn green when exposed to oxygen in the air is called

___ ___ ___ ___ ___ ___ ___ ___ ___ .
25   −9   72   17   35   2   72   25   −20

Use the order of operations to solve each problem below.

1. $4(6 - 2) + 2(3^2 - 9)$

2. $\dfrac{1}{4} \times 4 - \left(\dfrac{2}{3} + 1\right)$

3. $42 \div 7 - (5 \times 2) + 10$

4. $(4^2 - 5 \times 2) + \left|-10\right|$

5. $(4 - 3) - 5^2 + (3 \times 2^2)$

6. $\left|-2 \times 9\right| - 3 \times (-3)$

7. $60 \div (-5 \times 2) + (-8 - (-2 + 7))$

8. $56 - 24 \div (-6) + 2^{-3}$

9. $5(2-3)^4$

10. $\left(5(3-8)\right)+2\times2^2$

11. $4+\sqrt{81}-(6\div2\div3)$

12. $8.1\times(-2+4)-4.2$

13. $2.5+5.2-3\times2$

14. $3^{-2}-4\dfrac{1}{3}\times3$

15. $9-(4-6)+(2\times5)$

16. $-|8\times2|-3^2+5$

Using the properties of exponents

The properties of exponents allow you to simplify expressions. For each property, let x and y be any real numbers and m and n be any integers.

- **Negative exponents:** To simplify an expression that has a negative exponent, write the reciprocal of the expression, using the opposite of the exponent. Stated algebraically, $x^{-n}=\dfrac{1}{x^n},\ x\neq0$.

    Examples: $3^{-2}=\dfrac{1}{3^2}=\dfrac{1}{9}$ $2^{-3}=\dfrac{1}{2^3}=\dfrac{1}{8}$

- **Multiplication:** When multiplying the same base raised to different powers, add the exponents. The base remains the same. Stated algebraically, $x^m\cdot x^n=x^{m+n}$.

    Examples: $2^3\cdot2^2=2^{3+2}=2^5=32$ $3^{-1}\cdot3^4=3^{-1+4}=3^3=27$

- **Power of a power:** When taking the power of a power, multiply the exponents. The base remains the same. Stated algebraically, $(x^m)^n=x^{mn}$.

    Examples: $(2^3)^2=2^{3\cdot2}=2^6=64$ $(3^{-1})^4=3^{-1\cdot4}=3^{-4}=\dfrac{1}{3^4}=\dfrac{1}{81}$

- **Power of a product:** When multiplying two different bases, each raised to the same power, the exponent applies to both bases. Stated algebraically, $(xy)^m=x^m y^m$.

    Examples: $(4\cdot2)^2=4^2\cdot2^2=16\cdot4=64$ $(3\cdot2)^4=3^4\cdot2^4=81\cdot16=1296$

- **Division:** When dividing the same base raised to two different powers, subtract the exponent of the base in the denominator from the exponent of the base in the numerator. The base remains the same. Stated algebraically, $\dfrac{x^m}{x^n}=x^{m-n},\ x\neq0$.

Examples: $\dfrac{5^4}{5^3} = 5^{4-3} = 5^1 = 5$ $\dfrac{2^3}{2^{-2}} = 2^{3-(-2)} = 2^5 = 32$

◆ **Power of a quotient:** When dividing two different bases raised to the same power, the exponent applies to each base. Stated algebraically, $\left(\dfrac{x}{y}\right)^m = \dfrac{x^m}{y^m}, y \neq 0$.

Examples: $\left(\dfrac{7}{2}\right)^2 = \dfrac{7^2}{2^2} = \dfrac{49}{4} = 12\dfrac{1}{4}$ $\left(\dfrac{2}{5}\right)^3 = \dfrac{2^3}{5^3} = \dfrac{8}{125}$

EXERCISE 2·27

Use the properties of exponents to rewrite each expression below. Write the letter of the problem above its value at the end of the exercise to complete the sentence. Some answers will be used more than once, although they may be expressed in a different form. Some answers will not be used.

S. $\left(2^3\right)^2$

L. $5^2 \cdot 5^0$

I. $\left(3^1\right)^{-2}$

H. $(2 \cdot 5)^2$

A. $\dfrac{3^3}{3^2}$

M. $\left(\dfrac{2^2}{3^2}\right)^3$

C. $\left(3^{-3} \cdot 3^5\right)^3$

F. $\left(5^2\right)^{-4}$

The cheetah, which is capable of reaching speeds of 70 miles per hour, is considered to be the fastest land animal. However, few know that the

$\underline{\quad}$ $\underline{\quad}$ $\underline{\quad}$ $\underline{\quad}$ $\underline{\quad}$ $\underline{\quad}$ $\underline{\quad}$ $\underline{\quad}$
2^6 $\quad 3 \quad$ $\dfrac{1}{9}$ $\quad 25 \quad$ $\dfrac{1}{5^8}$ $\quad 3^{-2} \quad$ $\quad 64 \quad$ $\quad 100$

is the fastest sea creature and can swim up to 68 miles per hour.

Use the properties of exponents to simplify each expression.

1. $\left(4^3\right)^4$

2. $3^{-2} \cdot 3^2$

3. $\left(\dfrac{8}{9}\right)^5$

4. $4^3 \cdot 4^{-4}$

5. $\dfrac{4^{-3}}{4^4}$

6. 6^{-2}

7. $\left(2 \cdot 3\right)^3$

8. $\dfrac{6^4}{6^2}$

9. $\left(\dfrac{5}{7}\right)^2$

10. 9^{-2}

11. $\dfrac{8^{-1}}{8^3}$

12. $2^3 \cdot 2^{-1}$

13. $\left(5^2\right)^4$

14. $\dfrac{9^7}{9^{10}}$

15. $\left(1^5\right)^8$

16. $\left(\dfrac{3}{4}\right)^3$

Patterns, expressions, equations, and inequalities

Number patterns

Identifying number patterns, the way numbers are related, often makes the most difficult math problems easier to solve. In order to find patterns, you must examine a list of numbers called a sequence and find a "rule" that applies to every number in the sequence. The numbers in the sequence are called the terms of the sequence. Consecutive terms of a sequence are the terms that follow each other, without any missing numbers. Below is a list of common sequences and procedures for finding the rule that relates their terms.

- **Arithmetic sequence:** An arithmetic sequence is a sequence of numbers that follows a pattern of adding or subtracting the same number to or from consecutive terms. The number that is added to or subtracted from each term is called the common difference. Following is an example of an arithmetic sequence: 3, 8, 13, 18, 23 . . . To find the pattern of an arithmetic sequence, find the common difference between each set of consecutive terms. The common difference in this example is 5. The pattern is that 5 is added to each consecutive term to get the next term.

- **Geometric sequence:** A geometric sequence is a sequence of numbers that follows a pattern of multiplying or dividing each term by the same number. The number that each term is multiplied or divided by is called the common ratio. Following is an example of a geometric sequence: 5, 10, 20, 40 . . . To find the pattern of a geometric sequence, find the common ratio of each consecutive term by dividing one term by the other. The common ratio in this example is 2. The pattern is that each consecutive term is multiplied by 2 to get the next term.

- **Exponential sequence:** Exponential sequences include any patterns that involve the use of exponents. Following is an example of an exponential sequence: 3, 9, 81 . . . To find the pattern of an exponential sequence, determine whether the terms are increasing or decreasing. In this example, the terms are increasing. Then try to multiply each term by a base raised to a power to test for a pattern. In this example, each term is raised to the second power to obtain the next term.

Not all mathematical sequences will fit into one of these categories. If a sequence does not, use the following strategies to help you find a pattern.

- Determine whether the terms are increasing or decreasing.
- If they are increasing, the operation may be addition, multiplication, or exponentiation.

- If they are decreasing, the operation may be subtraction or division.
- Examine the pattern. Use guess and check to find the terms of the sequence and the operations that can be used to find the next term.
- Remember that the rule you select must apply to all the terms in a sequence.

Find the pattern for each sequence below and describe the rule. Then use the rule to fill in the missing numbers.

1. 3, 6, 9, _____, _____, _____

2. 1, 3, 7, 15, _____, _____

3. 17, 12, 7, _____, _____, _____

4. $-\frac{1}{2}$, 0, $\frac{1}{2}$, 1, _____, _____

5. 50, 25, 12.5, _____, 3.125, _____

6. −4, −2, 0, _____, _____, _____

7. _____, 16, 64, _____, 1,024 , _____

8. $\frac{1}{3}$, $\frac{1}{9}$, $\frac{1}{27}$, _____, _____, _____

9. 1, 2.5, _____, 5.5, 7, _____

10. 0, 7, 14, _____, _____, _____

11. $\frac{1}{2}$, 1, 2, 4, _____, _____

12. 1, 1, 2, 3, 5, _____, _____

13. 1, 4, 9, 16, _____, _____

14. $\frac{17}{18}$, $\frac{14}{15}$, $\frac{11}{12}$, _____, _____, _____

15. $\frac{1}{2}$, $\frac{1}{4}$, $\frac{1}{8}$, _____, _____, _____

16. 10, _____, −6, −14, _____, _____

Writing expressions

Two types of expressions are commonly used in mathematics: numerical expressions and algebraic expressions. Numerical expressions such as 7 or $3 + 4 \cdot 5$ consist of numbers and operation symbols such as addition, subtraction, multiplication, and division. Algebraic expressions such as $7y$ or $3x + 4 \cdot 5$ consist of one or more variables (a symbol used to represent a number), and possibly numbers and other symbols. All expressions can be compared to a phrase. Being able to write expressions is the first step that allows you to relate algebra to your life and solve complex problems. Follow the guidelines below for writing expressions.

1. Pay attention to key words that may signify each operation. Note that there may be exceptions. Below is a list of words that correspond to each operation.

ADDITION	SUBTRACTION	MULTIPLICATION	DIVISION
Add	Subtract	Multiply	Divide
More than	Minus	Times	Quotient
Increase	Decrease	Twice, doubled, etc.	Split evenly
Combine	Less than	Of	Half, third, etc.
Sum	Difference	Squared, cubed, etc.	Group
Total	Fewer than	Product	Per
Plus	Take away	Factor	Out of

2. Substitute a symbol for the meaning of the word. *Add* signifies addition. *Of* signifies multiplication.

3. Write the symbols in the order in which they appear in the phrase. Be careful with tricky wording in subtraction expressions such as "less than." "5 less than n" is written as $n - 5$, because 5 is the number being subtracted.

4. Use parentheses when necessary. For example, "3 times the sum of x and 9" is written as $3(x + 9)$ because you must compute the sum of x and 9 before multiplying it by 3.

5. After you have written your expression using numbers and variables, read it back to yourself to check that the wording matches the phrase. If it does not, try again. Remember that key words serve only as guidelines.

   Example 1: The sum of 8 and y

♦ *Sum* means addition.
♦ This expression can be rewritten as $8 + y$.

   Example 2: Twice the difference of 4 and n

♦ *Twice* indicates multiplication and *difference* means subtraction.
♦ Because the difference of 4 and n must be completed before multiplying by 2, you must place $4 - n$ within parentheses.
♦ *Twice* means times 2. The expression can be rewritten as $2(4 - n)$.

Match each phrase on the left with its variable expression on the right. Then write the letter of each answer in the space above its problem number at the end of the exercise to complete the sentence. Some letters will be used more than once.

1. n minus 3

2. A number, n, squared plus 17

3. The sum of n and 12 divided by 5

4. 3 more than n

5. n split into 5 groups

6. 17 less than twice a number, n

7. 15 increased by n to the third power

8. 12 less than the total of n and 2

9. 15 more than the product of n and 5

G. $n \div 5$

E. $(n + 2) - 12$

S. $\dfrac{n + 12}{5}$

L. $15 + n^3$

O. $5n + 15$

R. $n^2 + 17$

B. $2n - 17$

A. $n - 3$

C. $n + 3$

___ ___ ___ ___ ___ ___ ___ ___ and
 3   4   2   1   6   6   7   8

___ ___ ___ ___ ___ ___
 6   9   5   5   7   8

are two popular board games that build vocabulary.

Write an algebraic expression for each phrase.

1. The sum of y and 3.5

2. x increased by the sum of y and 12

3. 9 more than n

4. 25 divided by the difference of x and 5

5. The difference of 4 and z

6. z plus 3 cubed

7. 5 times the sum of 8 and y

8. The total of x and 5.7

9. The quotient of 55 and c

10. 24 less than the product of 3 and y

11. y split into 6 groups

12. The difference of 7 and x divided by 10

13. The square of the total of x and 9

14. Half of twice d

15. A number, k, decreased by 10

16. 42 minus the total of q and 7

Evaluating algebraic expressions

Algebraic expressions consist of one or more variables and possibly numbers and operations. When a value is given for a variable, this value can be substituted for the variable in the expression and the value of the expression can be found. This process is called evaluating the expression. Follow the steps below to evaluate variable expressions.

1. Rewrite the expression by replacing each variable in the expression with the assigned value. Place the value of the variable within parentheses in the expression to help you avoid careless mistakes.

2. Remember to substitute the value every time the variable is in the expression. This may be more than once. Be sure to be accurate.

3. If there is more than one variable in the expression, double-check that you have replaced each variable with the correct value.

4. Perform the operations in the expression by using the order of operations. Once you have substituted the corresponding values for each variable, perform the order of operations to evaluate the expression.

Example 1: Evaluate $5x - 10$ if $x = 3$.

- Rewrite the expression by substituting 3 for x. $5(3) - 10$
- Evaluate this expression by using the order of operations. $15 - 10 = 5$

Example 2: Evaluate $x^2 + 2y$ if $x = -4$ and $y = 5$.

- Rewrite the expression by substituting -4 for x and 5 for y. $(-4)^2 + 2(5)$
- Evaluate this expression by using the order of operations. $16 + 2(5) = 16 + 10 = 26$

Evaluate each expression below by substituting the value for each variable. Then write the letter of the problem in the space above its answer at the end of the exercise to complete the sentence. Some letters will be used more than once. Some letters will not be used.

O. $4n + 15$, if $n = 3$

N. $\dfrac{m^3}{m^5} + 7.5m$, if $m = 2$

E. $9(y - 4)$, if $y = -2$

R. $45r + (-15r)$, if $r = \dfrac{2}{5}$

P. $c^2 + 10 \div 2$, if $c = 4$

D. $-\dfrac{6}{7}x - 5x$, if $x = -7$

S. $\dfrac{1}{4} + \dfrac{2}{5}x$, if $x = -5$

G. $\dfrac{100}{y} - (-2y)$, if $y = 10$

A. $\dfrac{25}{5} - (3y)$, if $y = 10$

V. $\dfrac{2}{3}(-n + n) - n^3$, if $n = 3$

The National Guard is a branch of the military, in each state, of which the

___ ___ ___ ___ ___ ___ ___ ___
30   27   −27   −54   12 $15\dfrac{1}{4}$ 27   12

of that state is the commander.

Evaluate each algebraic expression.

1. $3x + 25$, if $x = 9$

2. $3(z - 15) + 2z$, if $z = 10$

3. $\dfrac{50}{5y}$, if $y = 5$

4. $(2 - y)(y + 10)$, if $y = 15$

5. $4 - x^2$, if $x = 6$

6. $4y + 2x - 5y$, if $y = -6$ and $x = -9$

7. $12z + 2x$, if $z = 3$ and $x = -4$

8. $10x \div 5$, if $x = 3.5$

9. $4y - 2x + 3$, if $y = 8$ and $x = -3$

10. $2.5z - 4.6x$, if $z = 3$ and $x = 7$

11. $20 \div 2y + y^2$, if $y = 5$

12. $(-2)(4x) - 4 \cdot 7y$, if $x = 5$ and $y = -3$

13. $\dfrac{x}{2} \div \dfrac{y}{4}$, if $x = 1$ and $y = 3$

14. $\sqrt{x} + \dfrac{x}{4}$, if $x = 36$

15. $\dfrac{x^3}{x^2} - 6x$, if $x = 4$

16. $\dfrac{yxz}{4(5-2)}$, if $y = -4$, $x = -3$, and $z = 10$

Simplifying expressions by combining like terms

The parts of an algebraic expression that are separated by an addition or subtraction sign are called "terms." For example, the terms in the expression $2x + 6$ are $2x$ and 6. Sometimes expressions have terms that are alike, or similar. When two or more terms have the same variable raised to the same power, they are called *like terms*. Like terms vary only in their numerical coefficients. (A coefficient is the number in front of the variable.) If there is no number in front of the variable, the coefficient is understood to be 1. Combining like terms allows you to simplify an algebraic expression. Follow the steps below to combine like terms.

1. Identify the like terms in the expression.

2. Add or subtract the like terms, depending upon the operation in the expression.

3. Add, subtract, multiply, or divide the real numbers following the order of operations.

4. Rewrite the expression.

Example 1: $3x + 5x - 6$

♦ The like terms are $3x$ and $5x$ because they have the variable, x, in common.
♦ Add $3x$ and $5x$ for a total of $8x$.
♦ Rewrite the expression as $8x - 6$.

Example 2: $7y - 2y^2 + 10 - 5$

- There are no like terms. $7y$ and $2y^2$ are not like terms because they do not have the variable, y, raised to the same power. $7y$ is raised to the first power and $2y^2$ is raised to the second power.
- Subtract 5 from 10. The difference is 5.
- Rewrite the expression as $7y - 2y^2 + 5$.

Example 3: $6z - z - 7 + 3$

- The like terms are $6z$ and z.
- Because there is no coefficient in front of z, the coefficient is understood to be 1. Subtract $1z$ from $6z$. The difference is $5z$.
- Simplify $-7 + 3$, which equals -4.
- Rewrite the expression as $5z - 4$.

EXERCISE
3·6

Simplify each expression.

1. $5 + 2x + x$

2. $3t + 2 + 4 + 4t$

3. $3x^2 + x^2 - 9$

4. $7b - b - 6 + 7$

5. $8p + 15 - 10p$

6. $19q - 11 + 6q$

7. $15t + 6t - 9t$

8. $20w + 3r - 5w - 8r$

9. $24m + 3 - 12m - 19$

10. $20a + 14 - 9a$

11. $\frac{1}{2}x + 2x - 13$

12. $11n + 8n^2 - 10n^2$

13. $x^2 + 3x^2 - 10x$

14. $13n + 4u^3 + 12n$

15. $\frac{4}{5}w - 4\frac{1}{2} + \frac{2}{3}w$

16. $3\frac{1}{2}y - 1\frac{2}{5}y + 1\frac{3}{4}$

Using the distributive property

The distributive property allows you to simplify expressions in different ways and makes numbers easier to work with. The distributive property states that $a(b + c) = ab + bc$ and $(b + c)a = ba + ca$ where a, b, and c are real numbers. You can use the distributive property to simplify expressions as sums or products. Keep in mind that the distributive property can be used either with expressions that include only numbers and operations, or with expressions including numbers, operations, and variables. Below are examples showing the use of the distributive property in numerical and algebraic expressions.

Numerical expressions
Example 1: 3×53

- The distributive property allows you to express large numbers as the sum of two smaller numbers in order to make computation easier. In this example, rewrite 53 as $50 + 3$.
- Rewrite the expression in factored form as $3(50 + 3)$. Remember that when a number is outside the parentheses and no operation symbol is written, it is understood that you must multiply.
- Rewrite this expression in expanded form as $3(50) + 3(3)$. Take the number outside the parentheses and multiply it by each addend: 3×50 and 3×3.
- These multiplication problems can easily be done using mental math: $3 \times 50 = 150$ and $3 \times 3 = 9$.
- Add $150 + 9$
- The sum is 159.

Example 2: 6×74

- Rewrite 74 as $70 + 4$.
- Rewrite the expression in factored form as $6(70 + 4)$.
- Rewrite this expression in expanded form as $6(70) + 6(4)$. Multiply 6×70 which equals 420 and 6×4 which equals 24.
- Add $420 + 24$.
- The sum is 444.

Algebraic expressions
Example 1: $4(x + 10)$

- Rewrite this expression in expanded form as $4(x) + 4(10)$ because each term within the parentheses must by multiplied by 4.
- Multiply each term: $4(x) = 4x$ and $4(10) = 40$.
- This expression equals $4x + 40$.

Example 2: $-2(y + 5)$

- Rewrite this expression in expanded form as $-2(y) + (-2)(5)$.
- Multiply each term: $-2y + (-10)$.
- Change the addition sign to a subtraction sign because 10 is a negative term. This expression equals $-2y - 10$.

Example 3: $3(4 - n)$

- Rewrite this expression in expanded form as $3(4) - 3(n)$.
- Multiply each term.
- This expression equals $12 - 3n$.

Match each expression on the left with an equivalent expression on the right. Write the letter of each answer in the space above its problem number at the end of the exercise to complete the sentence. Some letters will be used more than once.

1. 7×59

2. 14×8

3. 4×82

4. $2(x + 15)$

5. $6(x - 7)$

6. $-8(x + 3)$

7. $-4(2 - x)$

8. $5(4x + 3)$

A. $4(80) + 4(2)$

D. $-8x - 24$

G. $-8 + 4x$

P. $20x + 15$

E. $-8x + 24$

I. $6x - 42$

B. $15x + 20$

M. $2x + 30$

R. $350 + 63$

H. $80 + 32$

The $\underline{}$ $\underline{}$ $\underline{}$ $\underline{}$ $\underline{}$ $\underline{}$ $\underline{}$ $\underline{}$ $\underline{}$

       6   5   3   8   2   1   3   7   4

is a layer of muscle that moves up and down as you breathe.

Simplify each expression by using the distributive property.

1. 5×68

2. $8 \times (-24)$

3. $4(x + 7)$

4. $2(t + 5)$

5. $7(3 - b)$

6. 3×98

7. $9 \times (-45)$

8. $4x(x - 6)$

9. -2×57

10. $-6(n + 3)$

11. $5(m - 7)$

12. $-3(4 - n)$

13. $y(3y - 6)$

14. $-7 \times (-83)$

15. $8(9 - y)$

16. $-2b(7 + b)$

Introduction to equations

An equation is a mathematical statement that shows two expressions are equivalent. Equivalent expressions have the same value. The expressions in an equation are related by an equal sign. The expression to the left of the equal sign has the same value as, or is equal to, the expression to the right of the equal sign.

> Example 1: $2 + 3 = 6 - 1$

The two expressions are equivalent because each expression equals 5.

> Example 2: $2 \times 6 = 24 \div 2$

The two expressions are equivalent because each expression equals 12.

When an equation contains a variable, the equation may be true or false, depending upon the value of the variable. A solution to an equation is a number that makes the equation true.

To determine whether a given number is a solution to an equation, follow the steps below.

1. Substitute the number for the variable in the equation.

2. Simplify each expression.

3. If the expressions are equivalent, then the number is a solution to the equation.

> Example 3: Determine whether $x = 15$ is a solution to the equation $x + 5 = 20$.

- Substitute 15 for x.
- Simplify $15 + 5$ as 20.
- Because each expression equals 20, $x = 15$ is a solution to this equation.

> Example 4: Determine if $y = 20$ is a solution to the equation $25 \div 5 + y = 50 - 30$.

- Substitute 20 for y.
- The expression on the left, $25 \div 5 + 20$, equals 25.
- The expression on the right, $50 - 30$, equals 20.
- Because the expressions are not equivalent, $y = 20$ is not a solution to the equation.

Determine whether each equation shown is true.

1. $4 + 5 = 8 + 1$

2. $6 - 10 = 2 \times 2$

3. $25 \div 5 = 8 - 3$

4. $49 \div 7 = -7 \times 1$

Determine whether each value given is a solution to the equation.

5. $3 \times 5 = n \div 2; n = 30$

6. $10 + 8 = 3y; y = 3$

7. $2 - x = 10 + (-14); x = -4$

8. $6(4 - a) = -6 + 12; a = 3$

9. $-3b = 12; b = 4$

10. $3.5x = 7; x = 2$

11. $x + 10 = 17; x = 7$

12. $13 - y = 4; y = 11$

13. $4t = 24; t = 7$

14. $x \div 8 = -7; x = 56$

15. $-2y + 7 = -26; y = 13$

16. $14 - \dfrac{10}{m} = 19; m = -2$

Solving one-step equations with whole numbers: addition and subtraction

An equation is a mathematical statement that shows two expressions are equivalent. Equations can be solved to find the value of the variable that will make the equation true. The value that makes the equation true is a solution to the equation. Follow the steps below to solve equations.

1. Isolate the variable by using the inverse operation. Inverse operations are opposite operations that undo the operations in the original equation. When you use the inverse operation, you must perform the same operation on both sides of the equation. This results in an equivalent equation that has the same solution as the original equation. Addition is the inverse of subtraction. Subtraction is the inverse of addition.

2. Solve for the variable by writing the expressions on each side of the equation.

3. Check your solution by substituting the value of the variable back into the original equation.

Example 1: $x + 5 = 15$

◆ Isolate the variable x in $x + 5$ on one side of the equation: in other words, try to get x by itself on the left side of the equation. In order to isolate the variable, you must do the inverse, or opposite, of adding 5. The opposite of addition is subtraction. Subtract 5 from each side of the equation as shown below.

$$\begin{array}{r} x + 5 = 15 \\ \underline{- 5 \quad -5} \end{array}$$

◆ Solve for the variable by writing out the expressions on each side of the equation. Notice that $5 - 5 = 0$, which isolates x on the left. On the right side, you are left with 10 because $15 - 5 = 10$.

$$\begin{array}{r} x + 5 = 15 \\ \underline{- 5 \quad -5} \\ x = 10 \end{array}$$

◆ Check your solution by substituting the value of the variable back into the original equation.

$$10 + 5 = 15$$

Because this is true, $x = 10$ is the solution to the equation.

Example 2: $y - 14 = 24$

◆ Isolate the variable by adding 14 to each side, because addition is the inverse of subtraction.

$$\begin{array}{r} y - 14 = 24 \\ \underline{+ 14 \quad +14} \end{array}$$

◆ Solve for the variable by writing out the expressions on each side of the equation.

$$\begin{array}{r} y - 14 = 24 \\ \underline{+ 14 \quad +14} \\ y = 38 \end{array}$$

◆ Check your solution by substituting the value of the variable back into the original equation.

$$38 - 14 = 24$$

Because this is true, $y = 38$ is the solution to the equation.

Solve each equation for the given variable. Write the letter of the variable in the space above its solution at the end of the exercise to complete the sentence. Some letters will be used twice.

1. $n + 13 = 20$

2. $j - 12 = 36$

3. $e - 6 = 10$

4. $h + 8 = 23$

5. $g + 24 = 42$

6. $i - 31 = 18$

7. $o - 9 = 15$

8. $t + 35 = 4$

In anatomy, a

___ ___ ___ ___ ___   ___ ___ ___ ___ ___
15   49   7   18   16   48   24   49   7   −31

allows only back-and-forth movement. The knee is an example.

Solve each equation.

1. $n + 24 = 30$

2. $m - 9 = 13$

3. $x + 51 = 82$

4. $c + 31 = 42$

5. $y - 19 = 20$

6. $b - 61 = 18$

7. $t + 7 = 41$

8. $n - 12 = 89$

9. $m - 11 = 62$

10. $a + 17 = 93$

11. $x - 81 = 29$

12. $y + 9 = 192$

13. $t + 55 = 99$

14. $m - 77 = 14$

15. $c - 82 = 123$

16. $c + 47 = 153$

Solving one-step equations with whole numbers: multiplication and division

Solving equations involving multiplication and division is similar to solving equations with addition and subtraction. Instead of using the inverse of addition and subtraction, you must use the inverse of multiplication and division. Use the steps below to solve one-step equations involving multiplication and division.

1. Isolate the variable by using the inverse operation. Inverse operations are opposite operations that undo the operations in the original equation. When you use the inverse operation, you must perform the same operation on both sides of the equation. This results in an equivalent equation, an equation that has the same solution as the original. Division is the inverse of multiplication. Multiplication is the inverse of division.

2. Solve for the variable by writing out the expressions on each side of the equation.

3. Check your solution by substituting the value of the variable back into the original equation.

Example 1: $2x = 24$

♦ When a variable and a number, called the coefficient, are combined without any operation symbols in between, it means the coefficient is multiplied by the variable. In this example, 2 is multiplied by x. Use the inverse operation of multiplication, which is division, and divide each side of the equation by 2 to isolate the variable.

$$\frac{2x}{2} = \frac{24}{2}$$

♦ Solve for x by simplifying the expressions on each side of the equation. $2x \div 2 = 1x$, which leaves $1x$ on the left side of the equation. Simply write x, because the coefficient 1 is implied. On the right side of the equation, $24 \div 2 = 12$. Therefore, $x = 12$.

$$\frac{2x}{2} = \frac{24}{2}$$
$$x = 12$$

♦ Substitute 12 for x in the original equation: $2(12) = 24$. Because this is true, $x = 12$ is the solution to this equation.

Example 2: $y \div 3 = 6$

♦ y divided by 3 is expressed by using the division sign. However, mathematicians often represent division in equations by using a fraction bar. This equation could also be written as $\frac{y}{3} = 6$. Isolate the variable by using the inverse operation of division. Multiply each side of the equation by 3.

$$3\left(\frac{y}{3}\right) = 6(3)$$

- Solve for y by writing the expressions on each side of the equation. y is on the left side and 18 is on the right side. Therefore $y = 18$.
- Check the solution by substituting 18 for y in the original equation: $18 \div 3 = 6$. Because this is true, $y = 18$ is a solution to this equation.

Solve each equation for the given variable. Write the letter of the variable in the space above its solution at the end of the exercise to complete the sentence. One letter will be used twice. One letter will not be used.

1. $2k = 18$

2. $\dfrac{a}{4} = 6$

3. $n \div 5 = 5$

4. $6g = 42$

5. $3d = 36$

6. $3e = 15$

7. $10i = 100$

8. $b \div 13 = 4$

9. $\dfrac{s}{14} = 5$

10. $\dfrac{o}{8} = 32$

Sodium bicarbonate is another name for

$\underline{\hphantom{xx}}$ $\underline{\hphantom{xx}}$ $\underline{\hphantom{xx}}$ $\underline{\hphantom{xx}}$ $\underline{\hphantom{xx}}$ $\underline{\hphantom{xx}}$ $\quad$ $\underline{\hphantom{xx}}$ $\underline{\hphantom{xx}}$ $\underline{\hphantom{xx}}$ $\underline{\hphantom{xx}}$.

52 24 9 10 25 7   70 256 12 24

Solve each equation.

1. $3x = 15$

2. $t \div 3 = 36$

3. $5y = 30$

4. $99 = 9x$

5. $c \div 4 = 24$

6. $14n = 84$

7. $81 = 9x$

8. $2b = 82$

9. $6n = 54$

10. $13w = 52$

11. $162 = y \div 18$

12. $60 = y \div 15$

13. $\dfrac{b}{7} = 7$

14. $\dfrac{m}{8} = 1$

15. $21 = \dfrac{c}{3}$

16. $11 = \dfrac{n}{11}$

Solving one-step equations with rational numbers: addition and subtraction

The steps for solving one-step equations with rational numbers are the same as the steps for solving one-step equations with whole numbers. The only difference is that when computing rational numbers, you may have fractions, decimals, and negative numbers in the equation. Follow the steps below to solve one-step equations with rational numbers.

1. Isolate the variable by using the inverse operation. Inverse operations are opposite operations that undo the operations in the original equation. Addition is the inverse of subtraction. Subtraction is the inverse of addition. Keep in mind that you must use the same operations on each side of the equation.

2. Solve for the variable by performing the operations and writing out the resulting expression on each side of the equation.

3. Check your solution by substituting the value of the variable back into the original equation.

Example 1: $n + \dfrac{5}{6} = 4$

- Isolate the variable by subtracting $\dfrac{5}{6}$ from both sides of the equation.

$$n + \dfrac{5}{6} = 4$$
$$\underline{-\dfrac{5}{6} \quad -\dfrac{5}{6}}$$

- Solve for n. On the left side of the equation, $\dfrac{5}{6} - \dfrac{5}{6} = 0$. You are left with n. On the right side of the equation, you are left with $4 - \dfrac{5}{6}$. Remember that when you subtract a fraction from a whole number, you must change the whole number to an improper fraction and find a common denominator.

$$4 = \dfrac{4}{1} = \dfrac{24}{6}, \text{ therefore } \dfrac{24}{6} - \dfrac{5}{6} = \dfrac{19}{6} = 3\dfrac{1}{6}; n = 3\dfrac{1}{6}.$$

- To check your solution, substitute $3\dfrac{1}{6}$ into the original equation.

$$3\dfrac{1}{6} + \dfrac{5}{6} = 3\dfrac{6}{6} = 4. \; n = 3\dfrac{1}{6} \text{ is the solution to this equation.}$$

Example 2: $-3 - y = 6.23$

- To isolate the variable, add 3 to both sides of the equation.

$$-3 - y = 6.23$$
$$\underline{+3 \qquad +3}$$

- On the left side of the equation, $-3 + 3 = 0$. You are left with $-y$. On the right side, $6.23 + 3 = 9.23$. You are left with $-y = 9.23$.
- Find the value of y, not $-y$. The negative sign means "the opposite of." The opposite of a negative number is a positive number. Find the opposite of each side of the equation. This can be done by multiplying $-y$ by -1. When you multiply each side of the equation by -1, you will find the solution: $y = -9.23$.

$$
\begin{aligned}
-3 - y &= 6.23 \\
\underline{+3 \qquad +3} & \\
-y &= 9.23 \\
(-1)(-y) &= (-1)(9.23) \\
y &= -9.23
\end{aligned}
$$

- Check your solution by substituting -9.23 into the original equation: $-3 - (-9.23) = 6.23$. $y = -9.23$ is the correct solution to this equation.

   Example 3: $x - (-4) = 12$

- Rewrite the problem using the definition of subtraction: subtracting a number is the same as adding the opposite. $x - (-4) = 12$ can be written as $x + 4 = 12$.
- Isolate the variable by subtracting 4 from each side of the equation.

$$
\begin{aligned}
x + 4 &= 12 \\
\underline{-4 \quad -4} &
\end{aligned}
$$

- Solve for x. x is on the left side of the equation and 8 is on the right side. $x = 8$.

$$
\begin{aligned}
x + 4 &= 12 \\
\underline{-4 \quad -4} & \\
x &= 8
\end{aligned}
$$

- To check the solution, substitute 8 for x in the original equation. Because $8 - (-4) = 12$ is a true statement, $x = 8$ is a solution to the equation.

EXERCISE

3·14

Solve each equation for the given variable. Write the letter of the variable in the space above its solution at the end of the exercise to complete the sentence. Some letters will be used more than once. One letter will not be used.

1. $p + 2\dfrac{6}{7} = 5$

2. $r - 7.32 = 6.14$

3. $t + (-4) = -12$

4. $6 = a - (-13)$

5. $17\dfrac{3}{4} = 6 + e$

6. $-2.5 + o = 8.45$

7. $n + 5\dfrac{2}{9} = -\dfrac{1}{10}$

8. $15 = -s - (-10)$

9. $-\dfrac{3}{5} + w = \dfrac{3}{5}$

10. $-1\dfrac{4}{5} = i + 2.6$

Thomas Edison once said, "Genius is 1%

| $\underline{\hphantom{xx}}$ | $\underline{\hphantom{xx}}$ | $\underline{\hphantom{xx}}$ | $\underline{\hphantom{xx}}$ | $\underline{\hphantom{xx}}$ | $\underline{\hphantom{xx}}$ | $\underline{\hphantom{xx}}$ | $\underline{\hphantom{xx}}$ | $\underline{\hphantom{xx}}$ | $\underline{\hphantom{xx}}$ | $\underline{\hphantom{xx}}$ | and 99% |

$-4\dfrac{2}{5}$ $\quad$ $-5\dfrac{29}{90}$ $\quad$ -5 $\quad$ $2\dfrac{1}{7}$ $\quad$ $-4\dfrac{2}{5}$ $\quad$ 13.46 $\quad$ -7 $\quad$ -8 $\quad$ $-4\dfrac{2}{5}$ $\quad$ 10.95 $\quad$ $-5\dfrac{29}{90}$

$2\dfrac{1}{7}$ $\quad$ $11\dfrac{3}{4}$ $\quad$ 13.46 $\quad$ -5 $\quad$ $2\dfrac{1}{7}$ $\quad$ $-4\dfrac{2}{5}$ $\quad$ 13.46 $\quad$ -7 $\quad$ -8 $\quad$ $-4\dfrac{2}{5}$ $\quad$ 10.95 $\quad$ $-5\dfrac{29}{90}$

EXERCISE
3·15

Solve each equation.

1. $b + 2.67 = 3.8$

2. $y - \dfrac{1}{3} = \dfrac{5}{6}$

3. $-20 = x - 13$

4. $-5.7 + a = 15.9$

5. $m - (-5.2) = 18.43$

6. $-3\dfrac{3}{8} = k - 8\dfrac{3}{4}$

7. $\dfrac{3}{5} + a = 4\dfrac{3}{10}$

8. $12.72 - r = 18.2$

9. $45 = 12.5 - n$

10. $-17 = -t - (-19)$

11. $7\dfrac{11}{12} + x = -2\dfrac{3}{4}$

12. $d - \dfrac{2}{9} = 8\dfrac{2}{3}$

13. $-8.9 = -23 - y$

14. $-24.1 = 25 - m$

15. $c + 23\dfrac{3}{7} = 5\dfrac{1}{5}$

16. $-k + (-10.23) = -6.7$

Solving one-step equations with rational numbers: multiplication and division

The steps for solving one-step equations with rational numbers are the same steps you use when solving one-step equations with whole numbers. Remember to use the rules for multiplying and dividing decimals, fractions, and negative numbers.

1. Isolate the variable by using the inverse operation to undo the operation in the original equation. Division is the inverse of multiplication. Multiplication is the inverse of division. Keep in mind that you must use the same operations on each side of the equation and that you cannot multiply or divide both sides of the equation by zero.

2. Solve for the variable by performing the operations and writing out the resulting expression on each side of the equation.

3. Check your solution by substituting the value of the variable back into the original equation.

Example 1: $\dfrac{2}{3}x = 12$

♦ Isolate the variable by using the inverse operation. Because $\dfrac{2}{3}$ is multiplied by x, you must divide both sides of the equation by $\dfrac{2}{3}$ to isolate the variable x. Dividing by a fraction is the same as multiplying by its reciprocal: change the division sign to multiplication and find the reciprocal of the original fraction. The reciprocal of $\dfrac{2}{3}$ is $\dfrac{3}{2}$. Then multiply both sides of the equation by $\dfrac{3}{2}$.

$$\dfrac{3}{2} \cdot \dfrac{2}{3}x = 12 \cdot \dfrac{3}{2}$$

- Solve for x by performing the operation and writing out the resulting expression on each side of the equation. On the left side of the equation, $\frac{3}{2} \cdot \frac{2}{3} = 1$. You are left with x. On the right side of the equation, $12 \cdot \frac{3}{2} = 18$; so $x = 18$.

$$\frac{3}{2} \cdot \frac{2}{3}x = 12 \cdot \frac{3}{2}$$
$$x = 18$$

- Check your solution by substituting 18 for x into the original equation. $\frac{2}{3}(18) = 12$. This is a true statement. $x = 18$ is the solution to this equation.

Example 2: $-\frac{y}{5} = -3$

- Isolate the variable by using the inverse operation. Because y is divided by 5, you must multiply each side of the equation by 5 to isolate the variable.

$$5\left(-\frac{y}{5}\right) = -3 \cdot 5$$

- Solve for y. On the left side of the equation, $5\left(-\frac{y}{5}\right)$ is the same as $-y$. On the right side of the equation, $-3 \cdot 5 = -15$. You are left with $-y = -15$. Remember that a negative sign in front of a variable means "the opposite of." The opposite of y, which is the same as $-y$, is -15. The solution is $y = 15$.

$$5\left(-\frac{y}{5}\right) = -3 \cdot 5$$
$$-y = -15$$
$$y = 15$$

- Check your solution by substituting 15 for y into the original equation. $-\frac{15}{5} = -3$. This is correct. $y = 15$ is a solution to the equation.

EXERCISE 3·16

Solve each equation for the given variable. Write the letter of the variable in the space above its solution at the end of the exercise to complete the sentence. Some letters will be used more than once.

1. $\dfrac{3}{5}n = 14$

2. $l \div 3.5 = 2.9$

3. $-17 = \dfrac{2}{7}r$

4. $e \div \left(-2\dfrac{3}{4}\right) = -3$

5. $-\dfrac{g}{7.2} = 8.4$

6. $1.2m = 2.4$

7. $-3.6d = 18$

8. $-\dfrac{2}{5} = \dfrac{o}{8}$

$\overline{\quad}$ $\overline{\quad}$ $\overline{\quad}$ $\overline{\quad}$ $\overline{\quad}$ $\overline{\quad}$
-60.48 $\;-59\dfrac{1}{2}\;$ $8\dfrac{1}{4}$ -60.48 $-3\dfrac{1}{5}$ $-59\dfrac{1}{2}$

$\overline{\quad}$ $\overline{\quad}$ $\overline{\quad}$ $\overline{\quad}$ $\overline{\quad}$ $\overline{\quad}$
2 $\;8\dfrac{1}{4}\;$ $23\dfrac{1}{3}$ -5 $8\dfrac{1}{4}$ 10.15

is known as the father of genetics because of his work with pea plants. Through his experiments, he described how the traits of living things are inherited.

Solve each equation.

1. $\frac{2}{5}d = 10$

2. $h \div (-3.2) = 10$

3. $-1.5m = 8$

4. $-\frac{7}{9}n = -5\frac{1}{6}$

5. $4.2 = \frac{n}{0.4}$

6. $\frac{p}{1} = -15.83$

7. $-\frac{1}{3}x = \frac{8}{9}$

8. $m \div 4.88 = 15.23$

9. $6.7 = t \div 2.4$

10. $4\frac{5}{6} = 2\frac{7}{8}x$

11. $-3\frac{1}{2}y = -5\frac{2}{3}$

12. $-9.3 = -\frac{m}{2.1}$

13. $\frac{k}{4} = 10.34$

14. $-0.5m = 2.2$

15. $-12.2 = -0.8r$

16. $-\frac{w}{1.04} = 3.9$

Solve each equation.

1. $-8m = 32$

2. $-3.21 = 5.89 + d$

3. $34 + p = 42$

4. $-\dfrac{y}{1.25} = 8.9$

5. $-14.2 = r - 3.4$

6. $25 = c - 62$

7. $\dfrac{x}{4} = -6.3$

8. $9h = 81$

9. $\dfrac{7}{8}t = -6\dfrac{2}{3}$

10. $-23.7 + t = 74.9$

11. $2 = y + 4\dfrac{1}{2}$

12. $-14 = \dfrac{4}{5}x$

13. $18 - n = -45$

14. $y - 56 = 102$

15. $p \div (-5) = 30$

16. $\dfrac{k}{7.3} = 13.8$

Solving two-step equations with whole numbers

Two-step equations differ from one-step equations in that two operations are required in order to solve them. Use the steps below to solve two-step equations.

1. Try to isolate the variable by adding or subtracting the same number to or from both sides of the equation. Remember that you must "undo" the operations that are in the equation.

2. Continue to isolate the variable by multiplying or dividing both sides of the equation by the same non-zero number. Use the inverse of the operation that is in the equation.

3. Solve for the variable.

4. Check your solution by substituting the value of the variable back into the original equation.

Example 1: $2x + 5 = 15$

♦ Use subtraction to undo "plus 5." Subtract 5 from both sides of the equation. You are left with $2x = 10$.

$$\begin{array}{r} 2x + 5 = 15 \\ \underline{-5 \quad -5} \\ 2x = 10 \end{array}$$

♦ Continue to isolate the variable by using the inverse of multiplication. Divide each side by 2. When you divide, you are left with $x = 5$.

$$\frac{2x}{2} = \frac{10}{2}$$
$$x = 5$$

♦ Check your solution by substituting 5 for x into the original equation.

$$\begin{array}{r} 2(5) + 5 = 15 \\ 10 + 5 = 15 \\ 15 = 15 \end{array}$$

This is true. $x = 5$ is the solution to this equation.

Example 2: $\dfrac{n}{5} + 3 = 7$

♦ Isolate the $\dfrac{n}{5}$ by subtracting 3 from both sides of the equation. Subtraction is the inverse of addition. You are left with $\dfrac{n}{5} = 4$.

$$\begin{array}{r} \dfrac{n}{5} + 3 = 7 \\ \underline{-3 \quad -3} \\ \dfrac{n}{5} = 4 \end{array}$$

• Isolate the variable by multiplying each side of the equation by 5. Multiplication is the inverse of division. You are left with $n = 20$.

$$\frac{n}{5} = 4$$

$$5\left(\frac{n}{5}\right) = 4 \cdot 5$$

$$n = 20$$

• Check your solution by substituting 20 for n into the original equation.

$$\frac{20}{5} + 3 = 7$$

$$4 + 3 = 7$$

$$7 = 7$$

$n = 20$ is the solution to this equation.

EXERCISE
3·19

Solve each equation for the given variable. Write the letter of the variable in the space above its solution at the end of the exercise to complete the sentence. One letter will be used twice. One letter will not be used.

1. $2t + 7 = 27$

2. $3l - 12 = 24$

3. $\dfrac{a}{4} + 9 = 11$

4. $\dfrac{n}{8} - 15 = 1$

5. $3s - 12 = 39$

6. $\dfrac{m}{3} - 24 = 17$

7. $\dfrac{r}{9} + 71 = 95$

8. $11o - 43 = 56$

9. $\dfrac{w}{13} + 14 = 27$

10. $7e + 9 = 121$

___ ___ ___ ___ ___ ___ ___ ___ ___ ___
169   8   10   16   216   123   16   12   9   128

was so named because 95% of its composition is water.

Solve each equation.

1. $4x + 6 = 18$

2. $\dfrac{h}{2} - 4 = 11$

3. $5y - 8 = 22$

4. $2n + 10 = 12$

5. $\dfrac{b}{3} + 4 = 12$

6. $3m - 9 = 9$

7. $\dfrac{m}{2} - 9 = 7$

8. $\dfrac{g}{5} - 15 = 20$

9. $7r + 12 = 61$

10. $9d + 11 = 11$

11. $8c - 15 = 17$

12. $\dfrac{h}{7} - 18 = 21$

13. $\dfrac{k}{6} + 11 = 51$

14. $8x + 16 = 80$

15. $\dfrac{t}{8} - 13 = 72$

16. $\dfrac{k}{9} + 10 = 19$

Writing equations

Writing equations from sentences is similar to writing expressions from phrases. However, when you write equations, you are writing two expressions that are equal to each other. Remember, equations always contain an equal sign. Some key words that are used to write expressions may also be used to write equations.

ADDITION	SUBTRACTION	MULTIPLICATION	DIVISION	EQUALS
Add	Subtract	Multiply	Divide	Is
More than	Minus	Times	Quotient	Are
Increase	Decrease	Twice, doubled, etc.	Split evenly	Was
Combine	Less than	Of	Half, third, etc.	Were
Sum	Difference	Squared, cubed, etc.	Group	Equals
Total	Fewer than	Product	Per	Will be
Plus	Take away	Factor	Out of	Gives

Use an equal sign for the key words to show that two expressions are equal.

Example 1: 4 minus a number is 32.

Pay attention to the key words in the problem. The key words here are "minus," which means subtraction, and "is," which means *is equal to*. Select a variable to represent the value you are trying to find. Let us call it n. The equation, then, is $4 - n = 32$. To find the number, follow the steps for solving equations. You will find that $n = -28$. Check the solution by substituting -28 for n in the equation. $4 - (-28) = 32$ is a true statement. $n = -28$ is a solution to the equation.

Example 2: Two times the quantity n plus 5 equals 46.

There are four key words here: "times" meaning multiplication, "quantity" meaning a group of or parentheses, "plus" meaning addition, and "equals" which, of course, means equals. Select n to represent the number. Write the equation $2(n + 5) = 46$. Follow the steps for solving equations to find the number. You will find that $n = 18$. Check the solution by substituting 18 for n in the equation. $2(18 + 5) = 46$ is a true statement. $n = 18$ is a solution to the equation.

Example 3: Miguel sold 10 more than twice the number of raffle tickets that James sold. Miguel sold 102 tickets.

There are two key words here: "more than," which means addition, and "twice," which means *two times*. Since the expression "10 more than twice the number of raffle tickets that James sold" is the same as 102, the expressions are equivalent. Select j to represent the number of tickets James sold. Write the equation $10 + 2j = 102$. Solve for j. You will find that $j = 46$. Check the solution by substituting 46 for j in the equation. $10 + 2(46) = 102$. The solution is correct.

Place the letter of the equation that models each sentence in the space above the number of the sentence in the blanks below. n represents the number in each equation. The name of the mathematician who first used the equal sign will be revealed. Some equations will be used more than once. Some will not be used.

1. The product of 4 and a number is 6.

2. A number divided by 4 equals 6.

3. The quotient of a number and 4 equals 6.

4. The sum of a number and 4 equals 6.

5. A number plus 4 equals 6.

6. Four times a number equals 6.

7. Four minus a number equals 6.

8. Twice the sum of a number and 4 equals 6.

9. Four less than a number equals 6.

10. The ratio of a number to 4 is 6.

11. Four more than twice a number equals 6.

12. One-fourth of a number is 6.

13. A number times 4 equals 6.

B. $n - 4 = 6$

E. $4n = 6$

S. $2n - 4 = 6$

T. $2(n + 4) = 6$

W. $n + 2 \cdot 4 = 6$

C. $4 - n = 6$

O. $n + 4 = 6$

R. $n \div 4 = 6$

D. $4 + 2n = 6$

| __ | __ | __ | __ | __ | __ | __ | | __ | __ | __ | __ | __ | __ | __ |
| 2 | 4 | 9 | 6 | 3 | 8 | | | 12 | 1 | 7 | 5 | 10 | 11 | 13 |

Write an equation to describe each situation below. Then solve each equation.

1. Three-fourths of the 500 students in the school are involved in the athletic program. Find the number of students in the athletic program.

2. Mike made twelve equal monthly payments for an entertainment system. The cost of the system was $2,520. What was Mike's monthly payment?

3. Milly and Tina are collecting donations for a walk to fight cancer. Together they raised $500. Tina collected four times the amount that Milly collected. How much money did Milly raise?

4. A square has a perimeter of 36 inches. What is the length of a side of the square?

5. Canned goods are on sale 6 for $4. Find the sale price of one can.

6. A cell phone plan charges $49.99 per month plus $0.05 for each minute over 300. Find the total monthly charge for 355 minutes.

7. Melissa saved $5 a week and now has $115. How many weeks did she save for?

8. Sam left for school at 7:40 a.m. Jim left 15 minutes earlier. What time did Jim leave for school?

9. An adult ticket for the movies costs $9.50. A ticket for a child costs $7. Shawn purchased two adult tickets and some tickets for children. The total cost was $40. How many children's tickets did Shawn purchase?

10. A dress regularly sells for $89.99. It is on sale for half the original price. Find the sales price of the dress.

11. A number decreased by −4 is equal to 8. Find the number.

12. Jen is 17, which is 3 more than twice her cousin's age. How old is Jen's cousin?

13. A classroom has desks for 28 students, which is twice the number of computer stations. Find the number of computer stations in the classroom.

14. A computer monitor was on sale for $219, which is $25 less than the original price. Find the original price.

15. Allison's test score exceeded the class average of 83 by 10 points. What was Allison's test score?

16. Maria has to read 50 more pages in order to finish a book that is 215 pages long. How many pages has Maria read so far?

Writing and solving proportions

A proportion shows that two ratios are equivalent. Proportions are helpful in finding a missing part when the other quantities of the ratio are known.

To write a proportion, follow the steps below.

1. Identify each ratio.

2. Write the ratio with all the known quantities first.

3. Write the second ratio with the unknown quantity. Label the unknown quantity x. When you write the second ratio, set it up in the same way as you did the first ratio. The same kind of quantity should be the numerator of both ratios. The same kind of quantity should be the denominator of both ratios.

4. Write an equal sign between the ratios to show that they are equivalent.

To solve proportions, follow the steps below.

1. Use cross-multiplication to multiply each fraction's denominator by the other fraction's numerator.

2. Simplify each to write a one-step equation.

3. Solve for the variable.

4. Check your solution by substituting your solution for the variable into the proportion. Each ratio should be simplified to the same value.

> Example 1: 15 students in the first-period pre-algebra class wore a baseball T-shirt and 13 other students in the class wore their school colors to the last pep rally of the school year. Suppose 165 students wore baseball T-shirts to the pep rally. Based on the first period pre-algebra class, how many students wore their school colors?

- The ratios compare the number to students who wore baseball T-shirts to the number of students who wore their school colors.

- The ratio of the known quantities is $\dfrac{15 \text{ students wore baseball T-shirts}}{13 \text{ students wore school colors}}$.

- The ratio of the unknown quantity is $\dfrac{165 \text{ students wore baseball T-shirts}}{x \text{ students wore school colors}}$.

- This proportion can be written as $\dfrac{15}{13} = \dfrac{165}{x}$. Notice that in each ratio, the number of students wearing baseball T-shirts is the numerator and the number of students wearing their school colors is the denominator. When writing proportions, the same kind of quantity must be written in the same part of the ratio.

- To solve the proportion, cross-multiply. $15 \cdot x = 165 \cdot 13$ or $15x = 2{,}145$

- Solve for x by dividing both sides of the equation by 15. $\dfrac{15x}{15} = \dfrac{2{,}145}{15}$; $x = 143$

- Check the solution by substituting 143 for x into the proportion. $\dfrac{15}{13} = \dfrac{165}{143}$; $15 \cdot 143 = 165 \cdot 13$. Each expression in that last equation is equal to 2,145.

- $x = 143$ is a solution to the proportion.

> Example 2: A small pickup truck travels 180 miles on 6 gallons of gas. How many gallons of gas will it need to travel 720 miles?

- The ratios in this problem compare miles traveled to the number of gallons of gasoline used.

- The ratio with the known quantities is $\dfrac{180 \text{ miles}}{6 \text{ gallons}}$.

- The ratio with the unknown quantity is $\dfrac{720 \text{ miles}}{x \text{ gallons}}$.

This proportion can be written as $\dfrac{180 \text{ miles}}{6 \text{ gallons}} = \dfrac{720 \text{ miles}}{x \text{ gallons}}$.

- Cross-multiply to solve this proportion: $180 \cdot x = 6 \cdot 720$ or $180x = 4{,}320$

- Solve for x by dividing each side of the equation by 180. $\dfrac{180x}{180} = \dfrac{4{,}320}{180}$; $x = 24$

- Check your solution by substituting 24 for x into the proportion: $\dfrac{180 \text{ miles}}{6 \text{ gallons}} = \dfrac{720 \text{ miles}}{24 \text{ gallons}}$; $180 \cdot 24 = 720 \cdot 6$. Each expression in that last equation is equal to 4,320.

- The solution $x = 24$ is correct.

EXERCISE 3·23

Solve each proportion below. Then write the letter of the problem in the space above its answer at the end of the exercise to complete the sentence. Some letters will be used more than once. Some letters will not be used.

R. $\dfrac{5}{7} = \dfrac{x}{35}$　　　　　　　　I. $\dfrac{10}{y} = \dfrac{70}{56}$

W. $\dfrac{13}{17} = \dfrac{n}{68}$　　　　　　　M. $\dfrac{21}{43} = \dfrac{63}{t}$

S. Tara and Stephanie collected 3 caterpillars from one tree in their backyard. There are 8 trees in their backyard. How many caterpillars can they expect to collect?

T. Two college textbooks cost Sammi $173. She has a total of 6 textbooks to buy. How much money can she expect to spend on textbooks?

A. Jason earned $216 in three months on his paper route. If he works 2 more months, find the total amount of money he can earn.

O. Frank spends $75 on groceries each week. How much money does he spend on groceries in one month (counting a month as four weeks)?

A proportion is true if

___　___　___
$519　52　$300

___　___　___　___　___　___ are equal.
25　$360　$519　8　$300　24

Solve each proportion.

1. $\dfrac{4}{5} = \dfrac{x}{15}$

2. $\dfrac{24}{52} = \dfrac{x}{13}$

3. $\dfrac{y}{11} = \dfrac{44}{121}$

4. $\dfrac{n}{41} = \dfrac{49}{287}$

5. $\dfrac{8}{t} = \dfrac{1}{8}$

6. $\dfrac{12}{18} = \dfrac{k}{108}$

7. $\dfrac{175}{245} = \dfrac{35}{m}$

8. $\dfrac{366}{278} = \dfrac{183}{r}$

Write and solve each proportion.

9. A machine takes 3 hours to make 9 parts. At this rate, how many parts can be made in 27 hours?

10. An astronaut who weighs 156 pounds on Earth weighs 26 pounds on the moon. How much would a person who weighs 30 pounds on the moon weigh on Earth?

11. At the movies, a large bucket of popcorn holds 20 cups of popcorn and contains 1,100 calories. The medium bucket contains 15 cups of popcorn. How many calories are in the medium bucket of popcorn?

12. Sarah went to three yoga classes last month and burned a total of 849 calories. How many calories would she burn if she took 5 yoga classes?

13. Carlos made $156 in two weeks at his part-time job at a gas station. How much money would he make in a year?

14. Ryan has played in the first 5 games of the baseball season. In those 5 games, he has a total of 6 hits. How many hits should he expect to have in a 35-game season?

15. There are 2 boys for every 3 girls in class. If there are 12 girls in class, how many boys are there?

16. The ratio of dogs to cats entered in a pet show is 3 to 5. If 40 cats are entered, how many dogs are entered?

Finding the percent of increase and the percent of decrease

The rate of change is a ratio that compares the amount of change to an original amount. The rate of change can be expressed as a percent by using the proportion $\dfrac{\text{amount of change}}{\text{original amount}} = \dfrac{n}{100}$.

The amount of change may be greater than or less than the original amount.

- If the amount of change is greater than the original amount, the percent of change is called the percent of increase. The percent of increase can be found by using the formula $\dfrac{\text{amount of increase}}{\text{original amount}} = \dfrac{n}{100}$.

- If the amount of change is less than the original amount, the percent of change is called the percent of decrease. The percent of decrease can be found by using the formula $\dfrac{\text{amount of decrease}}{\text{original amount}} = \dfrac{n}{100}$.

To find the rate of change follow the steps below.

1. Find the amount of change.

2. Identify the original amount.

3. Insert the known values into the appropriate proportion.

4. Solve the proportion.

5. Express the answer as a percentage, rounding to the nearest percent, if necessary.

> Example 1: The admission price for a theme park was $29.99 in 2011. In 2012, the price went up to $34.99. Find the percent of increase.

- The amount of increase can be found by subtracting $29.99 from $34.99. The amount of increase is $5.
- The original amount is $29.99.

- Insert the known values into the formula $\dfrac{\text{amount of increase}}{\text{original amount}} = \dfrac{n}{100}$ to get $\dfrac{\$5}{\$29.99} = \dfrac{n}{100}$.

- Solve the proportion by cross-multiplying and then dividing both sides of the equation by $29.99.

$$\$29.99n = \$500$$

$$\frac{\$29.99n}{\$29.99} = \frac{\$500}{\$29.99}$$

$$n \approx 16.67$$

- The percent of increase is about 17%.

Example 2: Because of the recent storm, the attendance at the middle school basketball game fell from a record of 850 people at the previous game to 740 at last night's game. Find the percent of decrease.

◆ The amount of decrease can be found by subtracting 740 from 850. The amount of decrease is 110.

◆ The original amount is 850.

◆ Insert the known values into the formula $\dfrac{\text{amount of decrease}}{\text{original amount}} = \dfrac{n}{100}$ to get $\dfrac{110}{850} = \dfrac{n}{100}$.

◆ Solve the proportion by cross-multiplying and then dividing both sides of the equation by 850.

$$850n = 11{,}000$$

$$\frac{850n}{850} = \frac{11{,}000}{850}$$

$$n \approx 12.94$$

◆ The percent of decrease is about 13%.

EXERCISE
3·25

Find the percent of increase or the percent of decrease in each problem below. Round the answer to the nearest percent. Place the letter of the problem in the space above is percent at the end of the exercise to complete the sentence. One answer will be used more than once. One answer will not be used.

Find the percent of increase.

M. 20 is increased to 25.   L. 18 is increased to 20.

C. 10 is increased to 20.   P. 30 is increased to 40.

Find the percent of decrease.

K. 25 is decreased to 18.   A. 25 is decreased to 20.

O. 12 is decreased to 10.   R. 9 is decreased to 4.

Christopher Columbus's journey to find a western route to China was inspired by

___ ___ ___ ___ ___   ___ ___ ___ ___ ,

25%   20%   56%   100%   17%   33%   17%   11%   17%

who lived about 200 years earlier.

Find each rate of change and label it as a percent of increase or a percent of decrease. Round your answer to the nearest percent.

1. 25 to 50

2. 12 to 4

3. 25 to 10

4. 10 to 25

5. 80 to 90

6. 12 to 8

7. 11 to 15

8. 15 to 11

9. 15 to 7

10. 23 to 24

11. 35 to 38

12. 12 to 13

13. A $15.99 CD is on sale for $12.99.

14. Last year Mike earned $48,000 annually. This year his salary is $50,000.

15. A condo sold for $224,000 five years ago. It sold for $199,000 last year.

16. The annual property tax on a $350,000 home in Pleasant Streams was $7,000 last year. This year the annual taxes are $7,340.

Solving one-step inequalities with integers: addition and subtraction

Solving one-step inequalities with integers is the same as solving equations with whole numbers. The only difference is that inequalities do not have an equal sign. Instead, the equal sign is replaced with an inequality symbol. Inequality symbols include > (greater than), < (less than), ≥ (greater than or equal to), ≤ (less than or equal to), and ≠ (not equal to).

Use the steps that follow to solve inequalities. To check the solutions to inequalities, you need to select numbers that satisfy your solution. With greater than and less than signs, the number in your solution will not satisfy the inequality. For example, if $x > 3$, 3 is not a solution to the inequality because x must be greater than 3. To check the solution to this inequality, you must select a number that is greater than 3 such as 4.

Example 1: $x + 3 \leq 7$

- Isolate the variable by using the inverse operation. The inverse of addition is subtraction. Subtract 3 from both sides of the inequality.

$$\begin{array}{r} x + 3 \leq 7 \\ -3 \; -3 \\ \hline \end{array}$$

- Perform the operations and write out the resulting expressions on each side of the inequality. On the left side of the inequality, you are left with x because $3 + (-3)$ is equal to zero. On the right side of the inequality, $7 - 3 = 4$. You are left with 4. Therefore, $x \leq 4$.

$$\begin{array}{r} x + 3 \leq 7 \\ -3 \; -3 \\ \hline x \leq 4 \end{array}$$

- Check your solution by substituting numbers of the solution set into the original inequality. Replace x with 4. $4 + 3 \leq 7$ or when simplified, $7 \leq 7$. This is true. Now take a value that is less than 4, such as 2. Replace x with 2: $2 + 3 \leq 7$. When simplified, $5 \leq 7$. This is true; therefore, x ≤ 4 represents the solution set of the inequality. It shows that any number less than and including 4 is a solution to this inequality.

Example 2: $y - 10 > -15$

- Isolate the variable by using the inverse operation. Add 10 to both sides of the inequality.

$$\begin{array}{r} y - 10 > -15 \\ +10 \;\; +10 \\ \hline \end{array}$$

- Perform the operations and write out the resulting expressions on each side of the inequality sign. On the left side, you are left with y. On the right, $-15 + 10 = -5$. Therefore, $y > -5$.

$$\begin{array}{r} y - 10 > -15 \\ +10 \;\; +10 \\ \hline y > -5 \end{array}$$

- Check your solution. Less than and greater than inequalities require you to select numbers that satisfy your solution in order to check your solution. The solution to this inequality is $y > -5$. This means that y is greater than -5; the solution does not include -5. Select a number that is larger than -5 and substitute that number in the original inequality. You may select any number that is larger than -5, such as -4. Insert that number in the original inequality. $-4 - 10 > -15$. When simplified to $-14 > -15$, this is a true statement. $y > -5$ represents the solution set of this inequality.

Solve each inequality. Write the letter of each inequality in the space above its solution at the end of the exercise to complete the sentence. Some letters will be used more than once.

H. $3 + x \geq -15$

O. $x - 2 < -20$

P. $3 + x > 21$

C. $x + 19 \geq 12$

L. $12 + x \leq 24$

Y. $x - 3 \geq -15$

T. $x + 7 \neq 10$

S. $4 + x < -12$

U. $x - 13 \neq -16$

A. $-28 < -12 + x$

In 1928 Alexander Fleming discovered penicillin by accident. He left a dish of

___	___	___	___	___	___	___	___	-
$x < -16$	$x \neq 3$	$x > -16$	$x > 18$	$x \geq -18$	$x \geq -12$	$x \leq 12$	$x < -18$	

___	___	___	___	___	___
$x \geq -7$	$x < -18$	$x \geq -7$	$x \geq -7$	$x \neq -3$	$x < -16$

bacteria uncovered and found that a mold killed some of the bacteria.

Solve each inequality.

1. $y + (-8) > 13$

2. $d - 6 \geq 7$

3. $x - 7 < 18$

4. $-19 + t \leq 29$

5. $m + 14 \leq -21$

6. $42 > -31 + h$

7. $-24 \neq n - 9$

8. $c - 15 < 3$

9. $41 + k \geq 31$

10. $52 \leq x - 15$

11. $t - 19 < 62$

12. $y + 37 \neq 92$

13. $-82 > r - 53$

14. $5 + d \leq -67$

15. $w + 17 \neq 17$

16. $p - 28 \geq 74$

Solving one-step inequalities with integers: multiplication and division

The steps used to solve one-step inequalities by using multiplication and division are the same as those for solving equations by using multiplication and division. However, there is one major difference. When you multiply or divide both sides of an inequality by a negative number, you must change the direction of the inequality symbol.

Example 1: $3x < -15$

- Isolate the variable by using the inverse of multiplication. Divide each side of the inequality by 3.

$$\frac{3x}{3} < \frac{-15}{3}$$

- x is isolated on the left side of the inequality because $3 \div 3 = 1$. On the right side, you are left with -5 because $-15 \div 3 = -5$. The solution is $x < -5$.

$$\frac{3x}{3} < \frac{-15}{3}$$

$$x < -5$$

- Check your solution by substituting values of x for x in the original inequality. Since x is less than -5, substitute a number less than -5 for x in the original inequality. If you substitute -6, $3(-6) < -15$. Because $-18 < -15$, $x < -5$ represents the solution set of this inequality.

Example 2: $-2x > 20$

- Isolate the variable by using the inverse of multiplication. Divide each side of the inequality by -2. Remember to change the direction of the inequality symbol.

$$\frac{-2x}{-2} < \frac{20}{-2}$$

- x is isolated on the left side of the inequality because $-2 \div -2 = 1$. On the right side, you are left with -10 because $20 \div -2 = -10$. Since you divided both sides of the inequality by -2, you must change the direction of the inequality symbol. The solution is $x < -10$.

$$\frac{-2x}{-2} < \frac{20}{-2}$$

$$x < -10$$

- Check your solution by substituting values of x for x in the original inequality. Since x is less than -10, substitute a number less than -10 for x in the original inequality. If you select -11, $-2(-11) > 20$. Because $22 > 20$, $x < -10$ represents the solutions to this inequality.

Example 3: $\frac{y}{7} \geq 6$

- Isolate the variable by using the inverse of division. Multiply each side of the inequality by 7.

$$7\left(\frac{y}{7}\right) \geq 6 \cdot 7$$

- Perform the operation and write out the resulting expression on each side of the inequality. On the left side, you are left with y because $7\left(\frac{y}{7}\right) = y$. On the right side, you are left with 42 because $6(7) = 42$.

$$7\left(\frac{y}{7}\right) \geq 6 \cdot 7$$
$$y \geq 42$$

- Because y is greater than or equal to 42, you should substitute 42 for x in the original inequality to check your solution, $\frac{42}{7} \geq 6$. When simplified, $6 \geq 6$ is a true statement. Also substitute a value that is larger than 42 for x in the original inequality. If you substitute 49 for y, you get $\frac{49}{7} \geq 6$ or $7 \geq 6$, which is also true. $y \geq 42$ represents the solutions to this inequality.

EXERCISE

3·29

Solve each inequality. Place the letter of the inequality above its solution at the end of the exercise to complete the sentence. One letter will not be used.

A. $4x < -20$

P. $-\frac{x}{3} \leq -10$

R. $-3x < 15$

S. $-8x \geq 16$

Z. $2x > 10$

E. $14x \geq -28$

I. $\frac{x}{3} \geq -10$

T. $\frac{x}{3} \leq 10$

Saturn's eighth main ring was discovered by NASA scientists with the aid of the

___ ___ ___ ___ ___ ___ ___

$x \leq -2$ $x \geq 30$ $x \geq -30$ $x \leq 30$ $x > 5$ $x \geq -2$ $x > -5$

telescope.

Solve each inequality.

1. $5n < -25$

2. $\dfrac{g}{6} \geq 36$

3. $m \div 10 > -40$

4. $48 \leq -8d$

5. $32 \neq -8y$

6. $c \div 9 > -72$

7. $-65 \geq 13x$

8. $-10y < 80$

9. $\dfrac{k}{6} \leq 9$

10. $-39 \neq k \div 3$

11. $15r > -60$

12. $14m > 70$

13. $\dfrac{t}{12} \neq -7$

14. $x \div 17 < -68$

15. $3h \leq 63$

16. $\dfrac{y}{5} \leq -90$

Graphing

Graphing on a number line

In addition to ordering numbers and visualizing operations with real numbers, a number line can be used to graph equations and inequalities. An equation is a statement that two quantities are equal. An inequality is a statement that two quantities differ.

To graph an equation such as $x = n$ where n is a real number on a number line, find the point on the number line that can be paired with n. Place a heavy dot on that point. This dot, which is a closed circle, is a graph of the equation.

For example, the graph of $x = 1$ is shown in Figure 4-1.

Figure 4-1

Before graphing an inequality on the number line, it is necessary to review the meaning of the inequality symbols.

- $x \geq 1$ includes 1 and all real numbers that are greater than 1. Remember that fractions and decimals are included in the set of real numbers.
- $x \leq 1$ includes 1 and all real numbers that are less than 1.
- $x > 1$ includes all real numbers that are greater than 1.
- $x < 1$ includes all real numbers that are less than 1.
- $x \neq 1$ includes all real numbers except 1.

To graph an inequality such as $x > n$, find the point on the number line that can be paired with n. Place either a closed circle or an open circle on that point, depending on the specific kind of inequality you are graphing:

- Use a closed circle when x is $\geq$ or $\leq$ a number.
- Use an open circle when x is $>$, $<$, or $\neq$ a number.
- Shade the number line in the direction of the numbers that are solutions to the inequality.

The graphs of the inequalities discussed above are drawn in Figure 4-2. If the variable is on the left-hand side of the inequality, the number line is shaded in the same direction as the inequality symbol.

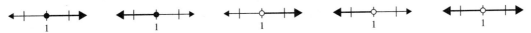

Figure 4-2

If the variable is on the right-hand side of the inequality, switch the number and the variable and reverse the direction of the inequality symbol. Rewriting an inequality in this manner produces an equivalent inequality, which is an inequality that has the same solutions as the original inequality. For example, $9 \leq x$ is equivalent to $x \geq 9$.

Example 1: Graph $x \geq -3$

+ Draw a number line and locate -3.
+ Place a closed circle on the number line on the point that is paired with -3. A closed circle must be used because the original inequality contains the $\geq$ symbol.
+ Since this inequality describes -3 and the real numbers that are greater than -3, shade the number line to the right. The graph is pictured in Figure 4-3.

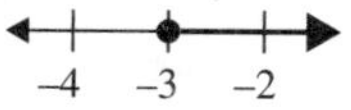

Figure 4-3

Example 2: Graph $x < 4$

+ Draw a number line and locate 4.
+ Place an open circle on the number line on the point that is paired with 4. An open circle is used because the original inequality contains the $<$ symbol.
+ Since this inequality describes the real numbers that are less than 4, shade the number line to the left. The graph is pictured in Figure 4-4.

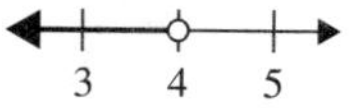

Figure 4-4

Example 3: Graph $2 < x$

+ Rewrite the inequality as $x > 2$ so that the variable is on the left-hand side of the inequality.
+ Draw a number line and locate 2.
+ Place an open circle on the number line on the point that is paired with 2.
+ Since this inequality describes the real numbers that are greater than 2, shade the number line to the right. The graph is pictured in Figure 4-5.

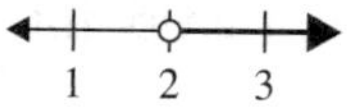

Figure 4-5

Consider the inequalities listed below. Write the letters of the inequalities that are graphed with an open circle and shaded to the right in the first three spaces at the end of the exercise. Write the letters of the inequalities that are graphed with a closed circle and shaded to the left in the last four spaces. Unscramble the letters to find the name of a state whose capital is not its largest city. Some letters will not be used.

M. $x < 7$

K. $5 \geq x$

E. $x > 3$

N. $x > -7$

I. $x \geq 0$

X. $x < 4$

R. $x \leq 0$

A. $5 > x$

B. $5 \leq x$

O. $x \leq -3$

Y. $x \leq -1$

W. $-3 < x$

___ ___ ___   ___ ___ ___ ___

Draw a separate number line for each problem. Graph each equation or inequality.

1. $a < 1$

2. $h \leq 3$

3. $4 \geq x$

4. $-5 > x$

5. $x > -3$

6. $-2 \leq b$

7. $n = 2$

8. $w \leq 3$

9. $x < -7$

10. $x \leq -5$

11. $-2 \geq c$

12. $5 = x$

13. $x \neq 0$

14. $y \leq -1$

15. $m < -4$

16. $-4 \neq x$

Graphing points in the coordinate plane

A horizontal number line, called the x-axis, and a vertical number line, called the y-axis, intersect at a point called the origin in the coordinate plane. The number lines divide the coordinate plane into four sections called quadrants. The quadrants are labeled counterclockwise, as pictured in Figure 4-6.

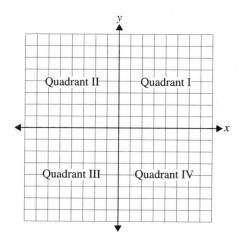

Figure 4-6

The number line and the quadrants make up the coordinate plane. It is used to graph ordered pairs, lines, and other relations. The graph of an ordered pair is a point in the coordinate plane.

To graph a point in the coordinate plane follow the steps below.

1. Start at (0, 0), the origin.

2. Consider the ordered pair (x, y).

3. The x-coordinate indicates how many units to move along the x-axis. If x is positive, move to the right. If x is negative, move to the left. If x is 0, do not move.

4. The y-coordinate indicates how many units to move along or parallel to the y-axis. If y is positive, move up. If y is negative, move down. If y is 0, do not move.

5. Place a dot on the point and label it with the coordinates of the ordered pair.

Example 1: Graph (3, –2)

♦ The first value, 3, is the x-coordinate. The second value, –2, is the y-coordinate.
♦ Start at (0, 0).
♦ Because 3 is positive, move 3 units to the right along the x-axis and stop.
♦ Because the y-coordinate is negative, move down 2 units, parallel to the y-axis.
♦ Place a dot in the coordinate plane and label it (3, –2). (See Figure 4-7.)

Example 2: Graph (0, 4)

♦ The first value, 0, is the x-coordinate. The second value, 4, is the y-coordinate.
♦ Start at (0, 0).
♦ Because the x-coordinate is 0, do not move along the x-axis. Because the y-coordinate is positive, move up 4 units along the y-axis.
♦ Place a dot in the coordinate plane and label it (0, 4). (See Figure 4-7.)

The graphs of both points are shown in Figure 4-7. Also included are the graphs of (−5, 3), (−4, −5), (−2, 0), and (6, 3).

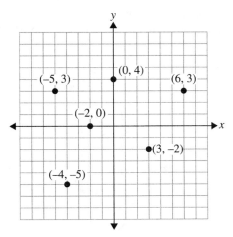

Figure 4-7

Graph the following points in the coordinate plane located below. If graphed correctly, a letter will be located next to each point that is graphed. Place the letter in the space above its ordered pair at the end of the exercise to reveal another name for graphing a point. Some letters will be used more than once. One letter will not be used.

1. $(0, 0)$

2. $(−4, 0)$

3. $(−5, 3)$

4. $(6, 3)$

5. $(−5, −3)$

6. $(3, −6)$

7. $(4, 0)$

8. $(−2, −5)$

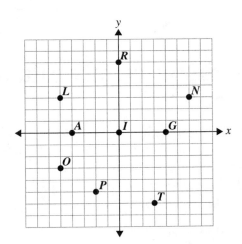

___ ___ ___ ___ ___ ___ ___ ___
(−2, −5) (−5, 3) (−5, −3) (3, −6) (3, −6) (0, 0) (6, 3) (4, 0)

___   ___ ___ ___ ___
(−4, 0)   (−2, −5) (−5, −3) (0, 0) (6, 3) (3, −6)

Several points are graphed in the coordinate plane pictured below. Match the letter of each point with its coordinates or description. When you are done, read down the column to find the name of the person who developed graphing in the coordinate plane. Some points will be used more than once.

1. ____ (0, 5)

2. ____ (0, 0)

3. ____ (−4, −1)

4. ____ The origin

5. ____ (−3, −6)

6. ____ The point where the axes intersect.

7. ____ (4, 0)

8. ____ (−2, 4)

9. ____ (6, 3)

10. ____ The only point graphed on the *y*-axis, other than the origin.

11. ____ (−7, 1)

12. ____ The point whose coordinates are neither positive nor negative.

13. ____ The only point graphed on the *x*-axis, other than the origin.

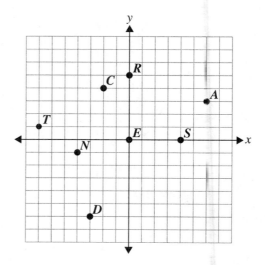

Using the distance formula to find the length of a line segment

A line segment is a straight line that has two endpoints. Graphing a line segment in the coordinate plane is easy if you are given the coordinates of the two endpoints. Just graph the endpoints in the coordinate plane and connect the points with a straight line.

To find the length of a line segment, use the distance formula, $d = \sqrt{(x_2 - x_1)^2 + (y_2 - y_1)^2}$, where *d* is the distance between the endpoints (x_2, y_2) and (x_1, y_1).

- Write down each endpoint and label one (x_2, y_2) and the other (x_1, y_1).
- Substitute the values in the distance formula.
- Use the order of operations to solve for *d*.
  - Simplify each expression within parentheses first.
  - Simplify the exponents.
  - Find the sum.
  - Find the square root.

Example 1: Find the length of the segment whose endpoints are (1, 4) and (2, 6).

♦ Sketch the graph of the line segment to help you visualize the segment. (See Figure 4-8.)

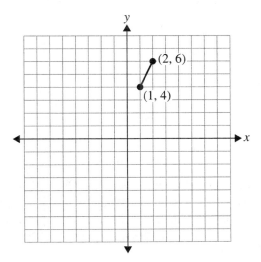

Figure 4-8

♦ Label (1, 4) as (x_1, y_1) and label (2, 6) as (x_2, y_2). Or you could label (1, 4) as (x_2, y_2) and (2, 6) as (x_1, y_1). This will not affect the answer.
♦ Substitute the value for each variable in the distance formula. $d = \sqrt{(2 - 1)^2 + (6 - 4)^2}$
♦ Simplify each expression within each set of parentheses. $d = \sqrt{1^2 + 2^2}$
♦ Simplify each exponent. $d = \sqrt{1 + 4}$
♦ Simplify the radicand, the number under the square root symbol. $d = \sqrt{5}$ or about 2.24 units.

Example 2: Find the length of the segment whose endpoints are (−4, 3) and (2, −1).

♦ Sketch the graph of the line segment to help you visualize the segment. (See Figure 4-9.)

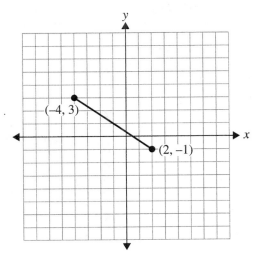

Figure 4-9

- Label $(-4, 3)$ as (x_1, y_1) and label $(2, -1)$ as (x_2, y_2). Or label $(-4, 3)$ as (x_2, y_2) and $(2, -1)$ as (x_1, y_1).

- Substitute the value for each variable in the distance formula. $d = \sqrt{(2 - (-4))^2 + (-1 - 3)^2}$

- Simplify each expression within each set of parentheses. $d = \sqrt{(6)^2 + (-4)^2}$

- Simplify each exponent. $d = \sqrt{36 + 16}$

- Simplify the radicand. $d = \sqrt{52}$ or about 7.21 units.

EXERCISE 4·5

Find the length of each line segment whose endpoints are indicated below. If you wish, you can sketch the graph of each line segment on graph paper. Write the letter of the problem in the space above the length of its line segment at the end of the exercise. Correct answers will reveal the name of a person who eats foods that have been locally grown. Some answers will be used twice. One answer will not be used.

L. $(0, 0), (5, 3)$ V. $(7, 3), (1, -4)$

A. $(3, 0), (8, 9)$ E. $(-1, -1), (1, -2)$

O. $(1, -2), (3, 6)$ G. $(3, -5), (1, 1)$

R. $(-4, -2), (-2, 0)$ C. $(0, 1), (2, 5)$

$\overline{\quad}$ $\overline{\quad}$ $\overline{\quad}$ $\overline{\quad}$ $\overline{\quad}$ $\overline{\quad}$ $\overline{\quad}$ $\overline{\quad}$ $\overline{\quad}$

$\sqrt{106}$ $\sqrt{34}$ $\sqrt{68}$ $\sqrt{20}$ $\sqrt{106}$ $\sqrt{85}$ $\sqrt{68}$ $\sqrt{8}$ $\sqrt{5}$

EXERCISE 4·6

Find the length of each line segment whose endpoints are listed below.

1. $(-4, 7), (2, 6)$

2. $(3, -2), (1, 8)$

3. $(4, -4), (1, 6)$

4. $(5, 1), (-5, -7)$

5. $(-2, 0), (10, -14)$

6. $(6, 8), (0, 2)$

7. $(0, 0), (5, 4)$

8. $(-6, 5), (0, -7)$

9. $(-4, 3), (2, -5)$

10. $(7, 1), (3, 7)$

11. $(5, 5), (0, -4)$

12. $(1, 1), (2, 1)$

13. $(-7, 2), (-7, 5)$

14. $(4, -8), (7, -3)$

15. $(4, 0), (4, -7)$

16. $(-2, -1), (4, 2)$

Finding the slope of a line

The slope of a straight line can be found by selecting two points on the line and finding the ratio of the change in the y-coordinates to the change in the x-coordinates. The formula for finding the slope of a line is $m = \dfrac{(y_2 - y_1)}{(x_2 - x_1)}, (x_2 \neq x_1)$.

Follow the steps below to find the slope of a line.

1. Select two points on the line.

2. Label one point (x_1, y_1) and the other point (x_2, y_2).

3. Substitute the values of the coordinates you have selected for the variables in the formula.

4. Simplify the result.

   Example 1: Find the slope of the line that contains the points $(-2, 5)$ and $(-1, 0)$.

   - Label $(-2, 5)$ as (x_1, y_1) and label $(-1, 0)$ as (x_2, y_2). You could also label $(-2, 5)$ as (x_2, y_2) and $(-1, 0)$ as (x_1, y_1). This will not affect the answer.

   - Substitute these values for the variables in the formula and simplify the result.

   $$m = \frac{0 - 5}{-1 - (-2)} = \frac{-5}{1} = -5$$

   - The slope of the line is -5.

Example 2: Find the slope of the line that contains the points (–3, 4) and (–3, 0).

- Label (–3, 4) as (x_1, y_1) and label (–3, 0) as (x_2, y_2). Or label (–3, 4) as (x_2, y_2) and (–3, 0) as (x_1, y_1).

- Substitute these values for the variables in the formula and simplify the result.

$$m = \frac{0 - 4}{-3 - (-3)} = \frac{-4}{0}$$, which is undefined. A sketch of the line that contains these points is a vertical line. Vertical lines have an undefined slope.

Example 3: Find the slope of the line that contains the points (1, 4) and (–2, 4).

- Label (1, 4) as (x_1, y_1) and label (–2, 4) as (x_2, y_2). Or label (–2, 4) as (x_2, y_2) and (1, 4) as (x_1, y_1).

- Substitute these values for the variables in the formula and simplify the result.

$$m = \frac{4 - 4}{-2 - 1} = \frac{0}{-3} = 0$$. A sketch of the line that contains these points is a horizontal line. Horizontal lines have a slope that is equal to zero.

EXERCISE
4·7

For each set of coordinates below, find the slope of the line. Write the letter of each point in the space above its slope at the end of the exercise to complete the statement. Some letters will be used twice.

T. (3, 4), (5, –2)   S. (0, 4), (4, 0)

H. (0, 0), (1, 2)   N. (–2, 1), (2, 6)

L. (6, –1), (–2, –3)   G. (4, 1), (5, 4)

I. (–1, –1), (–2, 4)   R. (1, 1), (4, 4)

A. (–1, 1), (3, –2)   E. (3, –4), (1, –1)

The slope of a

___ ___ ___ ___ ___ ___ ___ ___   ___ ___ ___ ___
-1 -3 1 $-\dfrac{3}{4}$ -5 3 2 -3 $\dfrac{1}{4}$ -5 $\dfrac{5}{4}$ $-\dfrac{3}{2}$

is constant.

For each set of coordinates below, find the slope of the line.

1. $(2, 5), (-4, 3)$

2. $(1, 4), (5, 0)$

3. $(0, 2), (1, 2)$

4. $(2, 1), (2, -7)$

5. $(5, -1), (-2, -2)$

6. $(-3, 1), (-2, 3)$

7. $(-4, 1), (-1, -4)$

8. $(2, 3), (4, 4)$

9. $(1, 1), (-3, -2)$

10. $(3, -3), (-1, -1)$

11. $(2, 4), (-6, 2)$

12. $(1, 4), (4, 0)$

13. $(-3, 0), (3, 2)$

14. $(-3, 1), (1, 6)$

15. $(0, -3), (-2, -3)$

16. $(4, 1), (-5, 4)$

Interpreting the slope as a rate of change

The slope can be used to visualize the rate of change of two different quantities. The rate of change represents the unit rate for a particular situation. The formula for finding the slope of a line between two points, $m = \dfrac{\text{change in } y}{\text{change in } x}$, can be modified to express a rate of change:

$\text{rate of change} = \dfrac{\text{change in one quantity}}{\text{change in the other quantity}}$. In this formula, the quantity that is represented by the y-coordinates is in the numerator. The quantity that is represented by the x-coordinates is in the denominator.

To interpret the slope as the rate of change, follow the steps below.

1. Express the data as two ordered pairs, writing one set of quantities as the x-coordinates and the other set of quantities as the y-coordinates. When determining which values represent the x-coordinates, think about which variable you would graph on the x-axis. Make these points the x-coordinates. Then think about which variable you would graph on the y-axis. Make these points the y-coordinates.

2. Substitute the values of your data for the variables in the formula. Note that the quantity that represents the y-coordinates is the numerator of this formula and the x-coordinates are in the denominator. rate of change $= \dfrac{\text{change in one quantity}}{\text{change in the other quantity}}$

3. Simplify the numerator and denominator.

4. Include the proper units in the ratio.

> Example 1: A family is driving to an amusement park. They are keeping a record of the distance and the time they traveled. At the end of the first day, they had traveled 315 miles in 5 hours. By the end of the second day, they had traveled a two-day total of 800 miles in 11.5 hours. This can be represented by the ordered pairs (5 hours, 315 miles) and (11.5 hours, 800 miles).

• The formula for finding the rate of change can be written as the

  rate of change $= \dfrac{\text{change in distance traveled}}{\text{change in time}}$.

• The change in the distance traveled from the first day to the second day is 800 miles − 315 miles or 485 miles.

• The change in time from the first day to the second day is 11.5 hours − 5 hours or 6.5 hours.

• The rate of change is $\dfrac{485 \text{ miles}}{6.5 \text{ hours}} = 74\dfrac{2 \text{ miles}}{3 \text{ hour}}$. This can also be expressed as $74\dfrac{2}{3}$ miles per hour. This means that on average for every hour that has passed, the family traveled $74\dfrac{2}{3}$ miles. This also represents the slope of the line that contains the points (5, 315) and (11.5, 800).

> Example 2: Mike is trying to lose weight in order to wrestle in a lower weight class. His results are summarized in two ordered pairs: (week #1, 185 pounds); (week #3, 170 pounds).

• The formula for finding the rate of change can be written as the

  rate of change $= \dfrac{\text{change in weight}}{\text{change in weeks}}$.

- The change in Mike's weight is 170 pounds – 185 pounds or –15 pounds.

- The change in time is 3 – 1 or 2.

- The rate of change is $\dfrac{-15}{2} = -7.5$ pounds per week. Since the rate of change is a negative number, it is interpreted as a loss of 7.5 pounds per week.

EXERCISE 4·9

Find the rate of change for each situation described below. Write the letter of the problem in the space above its rate of change at the end of the exercise to complete the statement. Some answers will be used more than once.

V. a charge of $350 for 5 hours; a charge of $450 for 7 hours

Express the rate of change in charge per hour.

E. saving $350 in 4 years; saving $600 in 6 years

Express the rate of change in savings per year.

T. earning $35 for 3 hours of work; earning $80 for 6 hours of work

Express the rate of change in earnings per hour.

M. selling price was $200,000 in 2011; selling price was $175,000 in 2012

Express the rate of change in selling price per year.

Y. $32 for 4 tickets; $48 for 6 tickets

Express the rate of change in cost per ticket.

N. 15 calculators for 15 students; 30 calculators for 30 students

Express the rate of change in calculators per student.

I. 90 on test #1; 80 on test #2

Express the rate of change in grade per test.

S. $250 for 30 movie tickets; $300 for 50 movie tickets

Express the rate of change in cost per ticket.

The average human heart beats about

___	___	___	___	___	___	___
$2.50	$125	$50	$125	1	$15	$8

___	___	___	___	___	a minute.
$15	−10	−$25,000	$125	$2.50	

Graphing linear equations written in slope-intercept form

The graph of a linear equation is a straight line. The slope-intercept form of an equation is $y = mx + b$, which can easily be used to graph the equation in the coordinate plane. m represents the slope of the line and b represents the y-intercept, the point where the line intersects the y-axis. The coordinates of the y-intercept are $(0, b)$.

To graph a linear equation written in slope-intercept form follow the steps below.

1. Identify the slope and express it as a fraction.

2. Identify the y-intercept.

3. Locate the y-intercept on the y-axis.

4. Starting from the y-intercept, consider the slope and move according to the sign of the numerator and denominator.

   ◆ If the numerator is positive, move up. If the numerator is negative, move down. If it is zero, do not move.
   ◆ If the denominator is positive, move to the right. If the denominator is negative, move to the left. If it is zero, do not move.

5. Graph the point.

6. Draw a line through the point and the y-intercept.

There are two additional considerations.

◆ If the equation of the line is $y = b$, the slope of the line is zero. To graph this equation, draw a horizontal line through the y-intercept, parallel to the x-axis.
◆ If the equation of the line is $x = b$, the line has an undefined slope. The line intersects the x-axis at $(b, 0)$. Draw a vertical line through the x-intercept, parallel to the y-axis.

Example 1: Draw the graph of $y = -4x + 2$.

The coefficient of x, which is -4, is the slope of the line. The slope can be rewritten as $\dfrac{-4}{1}$. The y-intercept is 2. The coordinates of the y-intercept are $(0, 2)$. Starting at $(0, 2)$, move down 4 units and 1 unit to the right (which is the meaning of a slope of -4), ending at $(1, -2)$. Graph this point. Draw a line through $(0, 2)$ and $(1, -2)$. The graph is pictured in Figure 4-10.

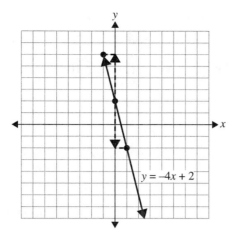

Figure 4-10

This equation can also be graphed by expressing the slope as $\dfrac{4}{-1}$. Starting at (0, 2), move up 4 units and 1 unit to the left, ending at (–1, 6). Drawing a line through (0, 2) and (–1, 6) produces the same line as illustrated above.

Example 2: Draw the graph of $y = -\dfrac{2}{3}x + 5$.

The slope, the coefficient of x, is $-\dfrac{2}{3}$, which can be rewritten as $\dfrac{-2}{3}$. The y-intercept is 5. Its coordinates are (0, 5). Starting at (0, 5), move down 2 units and 3 units to the right, ending at (3, 3). Graph this point. Draw a line through (0, 5) and (3, 3). The graph is pictured in Figure 4-11.

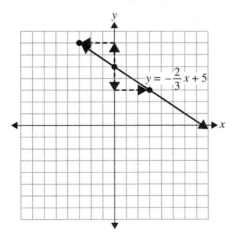

Figure 4-11

This equation can also be graphed by expressing the slope as $\dfrac{2}{-3}$. Starting at (0, 5) move up 2 units and 3 units to the left, ending at (–3, 7). Drawing a line through (0, 5) and (–3, 7) produces the same line as illustrated above.

Example 3: Draw the graph of $y = -2$.

The slope of this line is 0. The y-intercept is –2. Its coordinates are (0, –2). Draw a horizontal line through (0, –2). The graph is pictured in Figure 4-12.

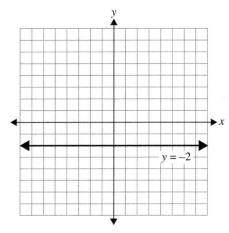

Figure 4-12

Example 4: Draw the graph of $x = 5$.

Although $x = 5$ is not in slope-intercept form, you can still graph this line. This line has an undefined slope. The line intersects the x-axis at (5, 0). Draw a vertical line through (5, 0). The graph is pictured in Figure 4-13.

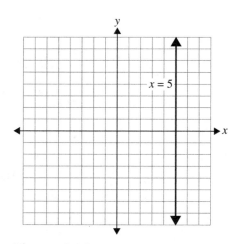

Figure 4-13

EXERCISE 4·10

Match each equation below with the lettered line in the graph that corresponds to it. Then place the letter of each line in the space above its problem number at the end of the exercise to complete the statement. One answer will be used twice.

1. $y = 2x + 3$

2. $y = 3x - 1$

3. $y = 4$

4. $y = -\dfrac{1}{2}x - 5$

5. $y = -3x$

6. $x = -7$

7. $y = x$

8. $y = -2x - 4$

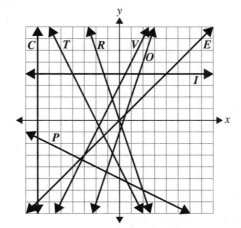

Since farmers are running out of land, a company in Texas has created

$\underline{\hphantom{xx}}$ $\underline{\hphantom{xx}}$ $\underline{\hphantom{xx}}$ $\underline{\hphantom{xx}}$ $\underline{\hphantom{xx}}$ $\underline{\hphantom{xx}}$ $\underline{\hphantom{xx}}$ $\underline{\hphantom{xx}}$ $\underline{\hphantom{xx}}$,
  1   7   5   8   3   6   5   2   4

a vertical farming system.

EXERCISE 4·11

Graph each equation.

1. $y = 3x$

2. $x = -5$

3. $y = -4x$

4. $y = 4$

5. $y = -x$

6. $y = x + 1$

7. $y = x - 2$

8. $y = 2x - 5$

9. $y = -2x - 5$

10. $y = x$

11. $y = \dfrac{2}{3}x$

12. $y = -\dfrac{2}{3}x$

13. $y = \dfrac{1}{4}x + 2$

14. $y = \dfrac{5}{4}x + 1$

15. $y = -\dfrac{1}{5}x - 3$

16. $y = \dfrac{1}{5}x - 2$

Solving systems of linear equations by graphing

A system of linear equations is two or more equations that have the same variables. When two equations are graphed in the same coordinate plane, the solution to the system is the point where the two lines intersect. Finding this point is called solving the system of equations.

To solve a system of equations, follow these steps.

1. Graph one equation, then the other using the method summarized below:
   - Begin with one of the equations expressed in slope-intercept form, $y = mx + b$.
   - Start at the y-intercept of one of the graphs and graph this point.
   - Move up or down, then right or left, depending on the slope and graph this point.
   - Draw a line through this point and the y-intercept.
   - Follow the same procedure to graph the other equation.

2. Find the point where the two lines intersect. (The point of intersection is the point where one line crosses the other.)

3. Write the coordinates of the point. This is the solution to the system of equations.

4. Check your solution by substituting the values of the coordinates of that point for the variables into both equations.
   - If the solution makes both equations true, it is a solution to the system of equations.
   - If the solution does not make both equations true, check your graph and your work again.

There are two additional considerations.

- A system may contain lines that have the same slope. Such lines are parallel and do not intersect. There is no solution to a system of equations that contains parallel lines.
- A system may contain lines that have the same graphs, meaning these lines coincide. Every point on the line makes both equations true. The system then has an infinite number of solutions.

Example 1: Find the solution to the following system of equations by graphing both equations in the coordinate plane.

$$y = x - 1$$
$$y = 3x - 5$$

- Begin with $y = x - 1$. The slope is 1, which can be expressed as $\frac{1}{1}$. The y-intercept is -1.

- Start at the y-intercept, -1, and graph this point. Since the slope is $\frac{1}{1}$, move up 1 unit and 1 unit to the right. Graph this point.

- Draw a straight line through these two points to graph the equation of the line.

- Now work with $y = 3x - 5$. The slope is 3, which can be expressed as $\frac{3}{1}$. The y-intercept is -5.

- Start at the y-intercept, -5, and graph this point. Since the slope is $\frac{3}{1}$, move up 3 units and 1 unit to the right. Graph this point.
- Draw a straight line through these two points to graph the equation of the line.
- The two lines intersect at $(2, 1)$, meaning that the solution to the system of equations is $x = 2$ and $y = 1$.
- Check your work by substituting $x = 2$ and $y = 1$ into each equation.

$$y = x - 1 \quad \rightarrow \quad 1 = 2 - 1$$
$$y = 3x - 5 \quad \rightarrow \quad 1 = 3(2) - 5$$

The graph of the two equations is shown here (Figure 4-14). The lines intersect at $(2, 1)$, which is the solution to the system.

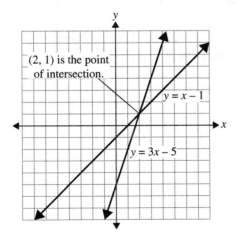

(2, 1) is the point of intersection.

$y = x - 1$

$y = 3x - 5$

Figure 4-14

Example 2: Find the solution to the following system of equations by graphing both equations in the coordinate plane.

$$y = x + 4$$
$$y = x - 1$$

♦ Graph each equation. Each has a slope that is equal to 1. The *y*-intercepts differ.
♦ When two lines have the same slope, they are parallel. Since the lines are parallel, they do not intersect. This system of equations has no solution.

The graph is shown in Figure 4-15.

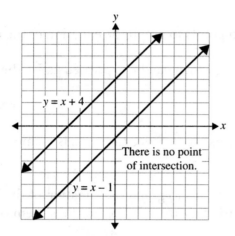

Figure 4-15

Example 3: Find the solution to the following system of equations by graphing both equations in the coordinate plane.

$$y = 2x - 1$$
$$y = 2x - 1$$

♦ Graph each equation. Note that each has a slope that is equal to 2. The *y*-intercepts are the same. Each is –1.
♦ The lines coincide. This system of equations has an infinite number of solutions. Every point on the line is a solution to the system of equations.

The graph is shown in Figure 4-16.

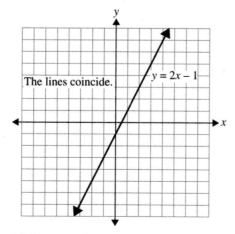

Figure 4-16

Solve each system of equations by graphing. Write the letter of the solution of each system in the space above its solution at the end of the exercise to complete the sentence. Some letters will be used twice. One letter will not be used.

E. $y = x + 1$

  $y = 3x - 7$

A. $y = 1$

  $x = 3$

S. $y = -x - 3$

  $y = 3x - 7$

R. $y = 3x - 4$

  $y = 3x + 4$

H. $y = -x + 6$

  $y = x - 4$

D. $y = -2x$

  $y = -3x - 3$

T. $y = 2x - 9$

  $y = 4x - 13$

V. $y = \dfrac{-2}{3} + 2$

  $y = -\dfrac{2}{3}x + 2$

L. $y = -\dfrac{1}{2}x - 1$

  $y = -x$

M. $y = \dfrac{1}{2}x + 4$

  $y = \dfrac{1}{2}x + 4$

Congratulations! You

___   ___   ___   ___

(5, 1)   (3, 1)   (0, 2)   (4, 5)

___   ___   ___   ___   ___   ___   ___

Infinitely many   (3, 1)   (1, −4)   (2, −5)   (4, 5)   No solution   (4, 5)   (−3, 6)

the point of this exercise.

Solve each system of equations.

1. $y = x + 5$
   $y = -2x + 8$

2. $y = x + 4$
   $y = -x + 6$

3. $y = 2x - 2$
   $y = 2x - 2$

4. $y = -1$
   $x = 1$

5. $y = 3$
   $x = 4$

6. $y = -x + 4$
   $y = -x - 1$

7. $y = x$
   $y = -x + 4$

8. $y = x - 1$
   $y = 2x - 3$

9. $y = 2x - 2$
   $x = 3$

10. $y = x$
    $y = -x$

11. $y = -x + 1$
    $y = -x + 3$

12. $y = -x + 1$
    $y = -x + 1$

13. $y = -\dfrac{1}{3}x + 2$
    $y = x - 2$

14. $y = -\dfrac{1}{4}x + 2$
    $y = x - 3$

15. $y = -\dfrac{2}{3}x + 2$
    $y = -2x - 2$

16. $y = -\dfrac{1}{2}x + 7$
    $y = -2x + 4$

Finding the *y*-intercept

The *y*-intercept is the point where the graph of a line intersects the *y*-axis. The value of *x* at any point on the *y*-axis is zero. This fact is used to find the *y*-intercept, given the equation of a line.
To find the *y*-intercept follow the steps below.

1. Substitute zero for *x*.

2. Then solve for *y*.

Example 1: $3x + 2y = 5$

- ◆ Substitute zero for x.
- ◆ Solve for y.

$3 \cdot 0 + 2y = 5$

$0 + 2y = 5$

$2y = 5$

$$\frac{2y}{2} = \frac{5}{2}$$

$y = 2.5$ The y-intercept is 2.5.

Example 2: $7y - 4x = -6$

- ◆ Substitute zero for x.
- ◆ Solve for y.

$7y - 4 \cdot 0 = -6$

$7y - 0 = -6$

$7y = -6$

$$\frac{7y}{7} = \frac{-6}{7}$$

$y = -\dfrac{6}{7}$ The y-intercept is $-\dfrac{6}{7}$.

Example 3: $y = 4x + 3$

This equation is written in slope-intercept form, $y = mx + b$, where b is the y-intercept. Just by looking at the equation you can immediately see that the y-intercept is 3. You may also substitute zero for x, then solve for y, to arrive at the same answer.

Example 4: $y = 8$

Since the variable x is not in this equation, the slope is zero. The graph of a vertical line has a slope that is equal to 0. The y-intercept of the line is 8.

Example 5: $x = -1$

Since the variable y is not in this equation, the line has an undefined slope. The graph is a vertical line that intersects the x-axis at −1. There is no y-intercept.

Find the y-intercept of each equation. Write the letter of each equation in the space above its y-intercept at the end of the exercise to complete the sentence. Some letters will be used twice. One letter will not be used.

A. $y = 3x - 1$

S. $y = 10$

E. $3x + y = 3$

Y. $3y + x = 3$

F. $2y = 4$

O. $y = 2x$

N. $x = -1$

D. $9x + 2y = -1$

I. $4y + 8x = 2$

L. $10x - 2y = 4$

Snow White and the Seven Dwarfs was called

_____ _____ _____ _____ _____ _____ _____   _____ _____ _____ _____ _____

$-\dfrac{1}{2}$ $\dfrac{1}{2}$ 10   none   3   1   10   2   0   −2   −2   1

by critics. They thought a full-length animated film would fail at the box office.

Find the y-intercept of the graph of each equation listed below.

1. $y = 2x - 1$

2. $y = x$

3. $y = 1$

4. $x = -4$

5. $2x + y = 0$

6. $x = y + 4$

7. $y + x = 3$

8. $4y = 2$

9. $3y = -9$

10. $x - 2y = 10$

11. $x + y = 7$

12. $x - y = 8$

13. $7x = 21$

14. $x = y - 6$

15. $y = \dfrac{1}{8}x + 2$

16. $y = -\dfrac{1}{3}x + 12$

Functions

Introduction to functions

A relation is any set of ordered pairs. A function is a special type of relation that pairs two quantities, the input and the output, according to a rule. For each input there is only and exactly one output. The domain of a function is the set of the input values. The range of a function is the set of the output values.

Example 1: Finding the perimeter of a square is an example of a function.

- The function rule states that the perimeter of a square is 4 times the length of one of its sides.
- The input values are the lengths of the sides of the squares.
- The output values are the perimeters of the squares.

Suppose you wish to find the perimeters of squares whose sides are 0.5, 3, and 10.

The input values are 0.5, 3, and 10. The output values are found by multiplying each input value by 4. If the side of a square is 0.5, the perimeter is 2. If the side of a square is 3, the perimeter is 12. If the side of a square is 10, the perimeter is 40. Note that each side of a square is paired with exactly one perimeter. The output values are 2, 12, and 40.

We can put this information into a function table as shown below. The input values represent the lengths of the sides and the output values represent the perimeters. This relation is a function because each input is paired with exactly one output.

INPUT	OUTPUT
0.5	2
3	12
10	40

Example 2. Finding the positive and negative square roots of a number is not a function.

- The rule states that the square root of a number is found by asking what number multiplied by itself equals the radicand (the number within the radical symbol).
- The input values are the radicands.
- The output values are the positive and negative square roots of the radicands.

Suppose you wish to find the positive and negative square roots of 0, 1, and 4. The input values are 0, 1, and 4. The output values are found by finding the square root of each of the input values. $\sqrt{0} = 0$, $\sqrt{1} = 1$ and -1, and $\sqrt{4} = 2$ and -2. If a relation is a function, each input value must be paired with exactly one output value. Since for this relation, some input values are paired with two different numbers as their output values, finding the positive and negative square roots of a number is not a function. (1 is paired with two different numbers, 1 and -1; 4 is paired with two different numbers, 2 and -2.)

A table for this relation is shown here. Notice that the inputs 1 and 4 have two different outputs. This relation is not a function.

INPUT	OUTPUT
0	0
1	−1
1	1
4	−2
4	2

Example 3: Finding the absolute value of a number is an example of a function.

- The rule states that the absolute value of a number is its distance from 0 on the number line.
- The input values are the numbers within the absolute value symbols.
- The output values are the distances that the numbers are from 0.

Suppose you wish to find the absolute value of −2, 0, and 2. −2, 0, and 2 are the input values. $|-2| = 2$, $|0| = 0$, and $|2| = 2$. The output values are 2 and 0. Each input value is paired with exactly one output value. Although 2 is the output value of both 2 and −2, 2 is listed only once when you list the output values.

A function table for this relation is shown here. Each input has exactly one output; therefore, the absolute value of a number represents a function.

INPUT	OUTPUT
−2	2
0	0
2	2

Determine if each table represents a function

1.

INPUT	OUTPUT
5	5
6	7
7	9

2.

INPUT	OUTPUT
3	1
5	1
7	4

3.

INPUT	OUTPUT
15	−3
10	−2
5	−1

4.

INPUT	OUTPUT
−3	−1
−3	0
3	−1
3	0

5.

INPUT	OUTPUT
−12	−24
0	0
12	24

Evaluating a function

Functions are often defined by letters such as f, g, and h. The value of the function can be found by substituting the value for x into the function and using the order of operations to find the resulting value. Finding the value of a function is also referred to as evaluating a function. Functions are shown by the notation $f(x)$. This is read "f of x." In function notation, $f(x)$ does not mean multiplication. This notation is simply a way to name functions.

Example 1: If $f(x) = x + 2$, find the value of $f(-3)$.

- This example asks you to evaluate the function f when $x = -3$.
- Substitute -3 for x in the equation $f(x) = x + 2$.

$$f(-3) = -3 + 2$$

- Since $-3 + 2 = -1$, $f(-3) = -1$.

Example 2 : If $g(x) = 4x - 1$, find the value of $g(7)$.

- This example asks you to evaluate the function g when $x = 7$.
- Substitute 7 for x in the equation $g(x) = 4x - 1$.

$$g(7) = 4 \cdot 7 - 1$$

- Since $4 \cdot 7 - 1 = 28 - 1 = 27$, $g(7) = 27$.

EXERCISE 5·2

Evaluate the functions for the given values. Write the letter of the problem in the space above the value of the function at the end of the exercise to complete the sentence. Some letters will be used more than once. One letter will not be used.

$$f(x) = x^2 \qquad g(x) = x - 4 \qquad h(x) = -2x + 5$$

R. $f(2)$ V. $f(0)$

P. $h(-3)$ O. $g(5)$

A. $g(-1)$ S. $h(0)$

B. $g(2)$ G. $f(-3)$

Y. $h(-1)$ K. $g(0)$

IBM's computer Deep Blue beat chess champion

___	___	___	___	___
9	−5	4	4	7

___	___	___	___	___	___	___	___
−4	−5	5	11	−5	4	1	0

in the first game of their match in 1996.

Find the value of each function at the given values.

$$g(x) = 3x^2 \qquad h(x) = -x + 2 \qquad f(x) = x - 1$$

1. $g(1)$

2. $h(2)$

3. $f(1)$

4. $g(-1)$

5. $h(-1)$

6. $f(2)$

7. $g(2)$

8. $h(1)$

9. $f(-1)$

10. $g(0.5)$

11. $h(-0.5)$

12. $f(1.5)$

13. $f(0)$

14. $g(-3)$

15. $h(-3)$

Finding the range of a function

The range of a function is the set of its output values. The range is commonly known as the *y*-values of a function. The range of a function can be found by inputting each member of the domain (the set of its input values) into the function and using the order of operations to simplify the expression. The domain is commonly known as the *x*-values of a function.

The domain of a function may be listed, or it may be included in an input-output table. If the domain is listed, then the range should be listed. If the domain is included in a table, the range should be included in a table.

Example 1: Find the range of $f(x) = 2x - 5$, if the domain is 3, 2, and −1.

- Substitute each member of the domain for x in the function $f(x) = 2x - 5$.
- Simplify each expression.

$$f(3) = 2 \cdot 3 - 5 = 1 \qquad f(2) = 2 \cdot 2 - 5 = -1 \qquad f(-1) = 2 \cdot (-1) - 5 = -7$$

- List the output values. The range is 1, −1 and −7.

Example 2: Find the range of $g(x) = -x + 1$. The domain, or x-values, is listed in the table below.

X	Y
3	
0	
−4	

- The domain is 3, 0, and − 4.
- Substitute each member of the domain for x in the function $g(x) = -x + 1$
- Simplify each expression.

$$g(3) = -3 + 1 = -2 \qquad g(0) = -0 + 1 = 1 \qquad g(-4) = -(-4) + 1 = 4 + 1 = 5$$

- Place the values in the table as shown. The range is −2, 1, and 5.

X	Y
3	−2
0	1
−4	5

The input-output tables may be written vertically or horizontally. The table above represents the same information as the table below.

x	3	0	−4
y	−2	1	5

Match each domain and function on the left with their range on the right. Write the letter of the range in the space above the number of the domain and the function at the end of the exercise to complete the sentence. One letter will be used twice.

1. $(3, 4, 5)$; $f(x) = x$

2. $(-3, 0, 3)$; $g(x) = \dfrac{x}{3}$

3. $(-6, -4, -2)$; $h(x) = 2x$

4. $(3, 4, 6)$; $f(x) = -x$

5. $(-3, 0, 3)$; $g(x) = x^3$

6. $(-1, 0, 1)$; $h(x) = (-x)^2$

7. $(-3, -1, 1)$; $f(x) = -2(x - 1)$

8. $(-3, 4, 5)$; $f(x) = -x - 5$

9. $(-3, -1, 1)$; $h(x) = 2(x - 1)$

B. $(-2, -9, -10)$

M. $(8, 4, 0)$

E. $(-8, -4, 0)$

O. $(-1, 0, 1)$

R. $(1, 0)$

K. $(-12, -8, -4)$

S. $(3, 4, 5)$

A. $(-3, -4, -6)$

T. $(-27, 0, 27)$

____ ____ ____ ____
 8   6   4   7

____ ____ ____ ____ ____ ____,
 1   5   2   3   9   6

author of the novel *Dracula*, wrote his first horror story at the age of twenty-eight.

Find the range of each function below with the given domain.

$$f(x) = x + 5 \qquad g(x) = 3x - 4 \qquad h(x) = 3x^2 \qquad F(x) = \frac{x}{2}$$

1. $f(x)$; the domain is 5, 0, −5.

2. $g(x)$; the domain is 5, 0, −5.

3. $h(x)$; the domain is 5, 0, −5.

4. $F(x)$; the domain is 1, 2, 3.

5. $g(x)$; the domain is 1, 2, 3.

6. $h(x)$; the domain is 1, 2, 3.

7. $f(x)$

X	Y
−10	
−8	
−2	

8. $g(x)$

X	Y
−10	
−8	
−2	

9. $h(x)$

X	Y
−10	
−8	
−2	

10. $F(x)$

x	3	6	8
y			

11. $f(x)$

x	3	6	8
y			

12. $h(x)$

x	3	6	8
y			

13. $g(x)$

x	3	6	9
y			

14. $g(x)$

x	−3	−6	−9
y			

15. $F(x)$

x	2	2	4
y			

16. $F(x)$

x	−2	−1	−4
y			

Finding the rule

A function is a rule that pairs each member of the domain with exactly one member of the range. If you are given a domain and a range, you can find the rule that pairs the numbers of the domain with the numbers in the range. Follow the guidelines below.

1. Look at the numbers in the domain and range to see how they are related.

2. Make a conjecture.

3. Test the conjecture on every member of the domain. Every member of the domain should be paired with a member of the range, using the rule.
   - If every member of the domain is paired with the corresponding member of the range, you have found the rule.
   - If the rule does not apply to each member of the domain, go back to step 1 and try again.

Example 1: Find the rule that pairs 2, 4, 6, with 3, 7, 11.

- The members of the domain are 2, 4, and 6. The members of the range are 3, 7, and 11.
- By looking at 2 and 3, the rule may be that 1 is added to the members of the domain. This can be expressed as $x + 1$.
- But this rule does not pair 4 with 7 because $4 + 1$ equals 5, not 7. The rule has to be revised.
- By thinking of the multiplication facts, notice that the members of the range are 1 less than 2 times the members of the domain. The rule may be $2x - 1$.
- Test the rule on each member of the domain. $2 \cdot 2 - 1 = 3$, $2 \cdot 4 - 1 = 7$, and $2 \cdot 6 - 1 = 11$.
- The rule is $2x - 1$. This can be written in function notation as $f(x) = 2x - 1$.

Example 2: Find the rule that pairs the values in the table.

x	−20	0	4
y	−5	0	1

- The members of the domain are –20, 0, and 4. The members of the range are –5, 0, and 1.
- By looking at the relationship between –20 and –5, the rule may be that the members of the domain are divided by 4.
- Test the rule on the other members of the domain. $0 \div 4 = 0$ and $4 \div 4 = 1$.
- The rule is $x \div 4$, which can be written as $\dfrac{x}{4}$ or $\dfrac{1}{4}x$. In function notation, this rule can be written as $f(x) = \dfrac{x}{4}$.

EXERCISE

5·6

Find the rule that relates the domain to the range. Write the letter of the rule in the space above the number of its domain and range at the end of the exercise to complete the statement. Some letters will be used twice.

DOMAIN	RANGE	RULE
1. 2, 3, 5	–2, –3, –5	G. x^2
2. 2, 4, 8	$\dfrac{1}{2}, \dfrac{1}{4}, \dfrac{1}{8}$	F. $-x$
3. –4, –3, –2	0, 1, 2	L. $3x$
4. –3, 0, 2	9, 0, 4	M. $-x^2$
5. 3, 1, –1	5, 1, –3	N. $2x - 1$
6. 0, 2, 4	0, 3, 6	Y. $4 + x$
7. 0, 2, 4	–4, –2, 0	T. $x - 4$
8. 1, 3, 9	3, 9, 27	I. $\dfrac{3}{2}x$
9. –1, 1, 3	–1, –9	A. $-2x + 1$
10. –1, 0, 1	3, 1,–1	O. $\dfrac{1}{x}$

Olympic gold medalist Shaun White is nicknamed the

"___ ___ ___ ___ ___ ___
 1   8   3   6   5   4

___ ___ ___ ___ ___ ___"
 7   2   9   10   7   2

because of his hair color and the heights he reaches in his jumps.

Find the rule that pairs each member of the domain with exactly one member of the range.

	DOMAIN	RANGE
1.	$-1, 0, 1$	$-3, -1, 1$
2.	$-1, 0, 1$	$-\dfrac{1}{2}, 0, \dfrac{1}{2}$
3.	$2, 4, 7$	$3, 5, 8$
4.	$-4, -3, -1$	$-6, -5, -3$
5.	$\dfrac{2}{9}, \dfrac{1}{3}, -\dfrac{1}{3}$	$\dfrac{2}{3}, 1, -1$
6.	$-1, -\dfrac{1}{2}, 0$	$1, \dfrac{1}{4}, 0$
7.	$\dfrac{1}{3}, \dfrac{1}{2}, 2$	$3, 2, \dfrac{1}{2}$
8.	$5, -1, -6$	$2, -4, -9$

9.

X	Y
0	2
−1	−2
−2	−6

10.

X	Y
−2	−16
0	0
2	16

11.

X	Y
−3	−27
−2	−8
−1	−1

12.

X	Y
−1	−3
−2	−2
−3	−1

13. _____

x	−2	1	3
y	−18	9	27

14. _____

x	−4	−1	5
y	8	0.5	12.5

15. _____

x	−1	1	3
y	1	−1	−3

16. _____

x	−4	8	6
y	−3	3	2

Answer key

1 The basics: numbers and properties

1·1 Natural: −4, −10, 0.5, $\frac{19}{20}$; Whole: $-\frac{1}{3}$, −2, −5, 0.49

Integer: $-\frac{2}{5}$, 0.7, $\frac{7}{8}$; Rational: $\frac{1}{\sqrt{3}}$, π, $\sqrt{8}$; Irrational: 10, $-\frac{2}{3}$, $0.\overline{1}$, 7; Real: There are no

numbers that do not belong; Pythagorean Theorem

1·2 Natural: 5, 123; Whole: 5, 0, 123; Integer: 5, 0, −25, 123; Rational: 5, $-\frac{2}{3}$, 0, 0.67, −25, $0.\overline{4}$,

123, $\frac{9}{10}$; Irrational: $\sqrt{11}$; Real: 5, $-\frac{2}{3}$, $\sqrt{11}$, 0, 0.67, −25, $0.\overline{4}$, 123, $\frac{9}{10}$; Natural: 17, 84, 1;

Whole: 17, 84, 1; Integer: 17, 84, −55, 1; Rational: $-\frac{3}{13}$, 17, 84, $-\frac{25}{26}$, −0.45, −55, 1; Irrational:

$\sqrt{23}$, π; Real: $-\frac{3}{13}$, 17, $\sqrt{23}$, 84, $-\frac{25}{26}$, −0.45, −55, π, 1

1·3 1.

2.

3.

4. 2 is larger than −5. Any positive number is larger than any negative number.

5. 3.5 is smaller than 4.5. 3.5 is located to the left of 4.5 on the number line.

6. $-1\frac{3}{4}$ is larger than $-3\frac{1}{2}$. $-1\frac{3}{4}$ is located to the right of $-3\frac{1}{2}$ on the number line.

1·4 1. 2   2. 7   3. −7   4. 2   5. $4\frac{3}{5}$ 6. −5.75   7. 8   8. −6   9. 1   10. −6.8

1·5 1. >, 3   2. <, A   3. <, I   4. ≠, L   5. ≥, 6   6. ≤, B   7. >, E   8. >, A   9. >, Y

10. >, A   11. =, I   12. <, 1   13. <, L   14. <, I   15. <, Z   16. >, Z 136 El Azizia, Libya.

1·6   1. −5, −3, −2, 0, 3; R   2. 25, 21, 18, 15, 14; T   3. −19, −10, 0, 1, 10; U   4. 3, 2, −2, −5, −7; E

5. −212, −101, −80, −75, −67; T   6. 20, 19, 18.5, 18, 17.5; M   7. $-1, -\frac{15}{20}, -\frac{4}{16}, \frac{4}{5}, \frac{9}{10}$; N

8. −10.9, −11, −11.1, −11.2, −11.$\overline{2}$; E   9. −2.$\overline{3}$, −2, −1.9, −1.8, −1; V   10. $3\frac{1}{3}, 2\frac{5}{7}, 1\frac{3}{5}, 1, -3$; C

11. $-1, -0.96, -0.95, -\frac{17}{18}, -\frac{6}{7}$; S   12. 2.01, 2, 1.$\overline{9}$, 1.99, 1.9; E Mount Everest

1·7   1. Addition property of zero

2. Multiplication property of zero

3. Associative property of addition

4. Associative property of multiplication

5. Commutative property of multiplication

6. Commutative property of addition

7. 135 = 135; commutative property of addition

8. 28 = 28; commutative property of multiplication

9. 27 + 4 = 12 + 19; 31 = 31; associative property of addition

10. 24 × 2 = 8 × 6; 48 = 48; associative property of multiplication

11. 30 + 8 = 25 + 13; 38 = 38; associative property of addition

12. 5 × 140 = 100 × 7; 700 = 700; associative property of multiplication

13. The grouping on the left; it is easier to add multiples of 5.

14. The grouping on the right; it is easier to multiply by multiples of 5.

2   Operations with rational numbers

2·1   G. 25   K. 86   I. −15   O. −18   R. −17   D. 47   L. 11   A. −27   F. −19   T. −16   E. 2€   P. −68
C. −23   M. 70   J. −9   H. −41   N. −36   B. −84   in the red; in the black

2·2   1. 9   2. −7   3. 15   4. −11   5. −20   6. 85   7. −36   8. −73   9. −45   10. −48   11. 94   12. 110
13. −74   14. −94   15. −153   16. −61

2·3   B. −2   U. 3   N. −8   L. −7   A. 6   F. −33   I. 4   C. 7   M. −10   S. −30   O. −11
D. −41   cumulonimbus

2·4   1. 4   2. −4   3. 14   4. 5   5. −6   6. 6   7. 2   8. 6   9. 2   10. −18   11. 23   12. −28   13. −43
14. −9   15. 0   16. 18

2·5   L. −9   M. 8   A. −3   K. 15   I. 4   J. −6   U. 7   T. 3   H. 9   F. 0   R. −10   B. −14   Burj Khalifa

2·6   1. 1   2. −1   3. 3   4. 2   5. −6   6. −5   7. −2   8. 2   9. −8   10. −12   11. −10   12. 24   13. 6
14. 9   15. −5   16. 16

2·7   B. 10   O. 29   U. −9   T. 44   N. 14   M. −57   D. −16   Q. −39   I. 16   A. 30   G. −22   S. −76
C. −23   L. −73   liquid, solid, gas

2·8   1. 8   2. −10   3. −17   4. −20   5. 27   6. 31   7. −22   8. −55   9. 72   10. 87   11. −129   12. 22
13. 100   14. −89   15. 57   16. −114

2·9   1. −49   2. −20   3. −18   4. 40   5. 60   6. −33   7. 60   8. −72   9. −17   10. 16   11. 165   12. −252
13. 102   14. 64   15. −63   16. 24

2·10   1. 5   2. −5   3. 6   4. 0   5. 7   6. −8   7. −9   8. 7   9. −9   10. Undefined   11. 12   12. −4
13. −13   14. 52   15. −11   16. 27

2·11 S. $-1\frac{19}{36}$ I. 0.49 H. −0.98 R. −5.8 C. $1\frac{3}{8}$ O. 5 A. $-\frac{29}{30}$ B. $-1\frac{1}{2}$ L. $2\frac{1}{9}$ T. $-5\frac{17}{30}$

  N. −2.5 M. $5\frac{17}{28}$ K. 13.45 U. $-3\frac{1}{10}$ Russia…million

2·12 1. −0.75 2. $\frac{31}{35}$ 3. $-\frac{7}{8}$ 4. −1.24 5. $-1\frac{4}{35}$ 6. 2.36 7. −3.8 8. $-2\frac{11}{21}$ 9. $5\frac{1}{12}$ 10. −4.3

  11. $-4\frac{1}{2}$ 12. 8.55 13. −5.8 14. $-6\frac{1}{4}$ 15. $-1\frac{2}{15}$ 16. $-3\frac{1}{12}$

2·13 N. −0.2 E. $\frac{19}{28}$ T. $\frac{3}{8}$ L. 2.45 I. $-\frac{2}{15}$ D. $4\frac{1}{10}$ C. −0.57 Y. −3.375 W. 2.2 R. −1.4

  M. $-1\frac{7}{12}$ B. $\frac{13}{15}$ Liberty Bell

2·14 1. −0.5 2. $\frac{5}{14}$ 3. 0.3 4. −1.3 5. $\frac{2}{15}$ 6. $\frac{1}{30}$ 7. 0.66 8. 0.49 9. $\frac{3}{4}$ 10. $\frac{7}{10}$

  11. −3.83 12. 0.57 13. $-1\frac{17}{22}$ 14. $-2\frac{3}{4}$ 15. 8.8 16. 1.3

2·15 A. $-\frac{3}{10}$ C. $-2\frac{5}{6}$ I. $-3\frac{1}{6}$ F. −1.87 E. 0.36 L. $13\frac{8}{9}$ D. −3.15 P. $-13\frac{7}{40}$ N. $-\frac{13}{20}$

  M. $1\frac{11}{14}$ lead pencil

2·16 1. $1\frac{5}{8}$ 2. $-\frac{8}{15}$ 3. −0.87 4. 1.33 5. −1.86 6. $-2\frac{1}{4}$ 7. $-\frac{29}{42}$ 8. −5.16 9. $-1\frac{9}{56}$

  10. $-2\frac{9}{20}$ 11. 0 12. $\frac{26}{45}$ 13. 24.45 14. $12\frac{41}{90}$ 15. −12.3 16. −2.7

2·17 1. $-\frac{7}{12}$ 2. 0.27 3. $-\frac{1}{15}$ 4. −3.12 5. $\frac{20}{21}$ 6. −1.2 7. $\frac{1}{36}$ 8. 8.28 9. $-6\frac{7}{8}$ 10. −5.282

  11. $\frac{27}{40}$ 12. $17\frac{1}{4}$ 13. −2.565 14. 0.12 15. $-\frac{16}{39}$ 16. 1.5

2·18 1. 4 2. $-\frac{8}{15}$ 3. $\frac{1}{3}$ 4. $\frac{32}{35}$ 5. −0.3 6. $\frac{3}{4}$ 7. 4 8. −2 9. $-7\frac{1}{2}$ 10. −9 11. 1.8 12. −30

  13. $1\frac{31}{49}$ 14. 5 15. $-4\frac{1}{2}$ 16. 2.25

2·19 A. −12 R. −29 D. 12 L. −15 E. −6 F. 27 I. 4 O. −31 S. −8 N. −24 P. 10
  T. 31 Leonardo of Pisa

2·20 1. −14 2. −40 3. −7 4. −21 5. −24 6. −5 7. −17 8. 6 9. −240 10. 20 11. 22 12. −36
  13. −18 14. 5 15. −6 16. −5

2·21 1. 3 2. 13 3. 16 4. −52 5. 50 6. 10 7. −12 8. −38 9. 0 10. 0 11. −6 12. 10 13. −15
  14. −3 15. 12 16. 36

2·22 1. 32, C 2. −1, I 3. 1, I 4. $\frac{1}{125}$, N 5. $\frac{1}{256}$, O 6. 216, S 7. −25, L silicon

2·23 1. 8 2. $\frac{1}{27}$ 3. 16 4. $-\frac{1}{16}$ 5. $\frac{1}{1,296}$ 6. 64 7. 1,000 8. −1 9. −64 10. 400 11. 343

  12. $\frac{1}{121}$ 13. 1 14. $-\frac{1}{3}$ 15. −32 16. $-\frac{1}{128}$

2·24 1. 6 2. 13 3. 2 4. 12 5. 8 6. 7 7. 3 8. 14 9. 1 10. 11 11. 5 12. 9 13. 10 14. 15
  15. 16 16. 4

2·25   D. 17   I. 72   T. 2   X. −9   B. 53   O. 25   A. 35   R. 51   N. −20   M. 21   oxidation

2·26   1. 16   2. $-\dfrac{2}{3}$ 3. 6   4. 16   5. −12   6. 27   7. −19   8. $60\dfrac{1}{8}$ 9. 5   10. −17   11. 12   12. 12

13. 1.7   14. $-12\dfrac{8}{9}$ 15. 21   16. −20

2·27   S. 2^6 or 64   A. 3   L. 25   M. $\dfrac{64}{729}$ I. 3^{-2} or $\dfrac{1}{9}$ C. 3^6 or 729   H. 100   F. $\dfrac{1}{5^8}$ sailfish

2·28   1. 4^{12} 2. 1   3. $\dfrac{8^5}{9^5}$ 4. $\dfrac{1}{4}$ 5. $\dfrac{1}{4^7}$ 6. $\dfrac{1}{6^2}$ or $\dfrac{1}{36}$ 7. 6^3 or 216   8. 6^2 or 36   9. $\dfrac{5^2}{7^2} = \dfrac{25}{49}$

10. $\dfrac{1}{9^2} = \dfrac{1}{81}$ 11. $\dfrac{1}{8^4}$ 12. $2^2 = 4$ 13. 5^8 14. $\dfrac{1}{9^3}$ 15. $1^{40} = 1$ 16. $\dfrac{3^3}{4^3} = \dfrac{27}{64}$

3   Patterns, expressions, equations, and inequalities

3·1   Explanations of patterns may vary.

1. The pattern is to add 3: 12, 15, 18

2. The pattern is to add the next consecutive powers of 2: 31, 63

3. The pattern is to subtract 5: 2, −3, −8

4. The pattern is to add $\dfrac{1}{2}$: $1\dfrac{1}{2}$, 2

5. The pattern is to divide by 2: 6.25, 1.5625

6. The pattern is to add 2: 2, 4, 6

7. The pattern is to multiply each previous term by 4: 4, 256, 4,096

8. The pattern is to multiply the previous term by $\dfrac{1}{3}$: $\dfrac{1}{81}$, $\dfrac{1}{243}$, $\dfrac{1}{729}$

9. The pattern is to add 1.5: 4, 8.5

10. The pattern is to add 7: 21, 28, 35

11. The pattern is to double the previous term: 8, 16

12. The pattern is to add the two previous terms: 8, 13

13. The pattern is to add consecutive odd numbers: 25, 36

14. The pattern is to subtract 3 from both the numerator and the denominator: $\dfrac{8}{9}$, $\dfrac{5}{6}$, $\dfrac{2}{3}$

15. The pattern is to multiply the previous term by $\dfrac{1}{2}$: $\dfrac{1}{16}$, $\dfrac{1}{32}$, $\dfrac{1}{64}$

16. The pattern is to subtract 8: 2, −22, −30

3·2   1. A   2. R   3. S   4. C   5. G   6. B   7. L   8. E   9. O   Scrabble and Boggle

3·3   1. $y + 3.5$ 2. $x + (y + 12)$ 3. $n + 9$ 4. $\dfrac{25}{x - 5}$ or $25 \div (x - 5)$ 5. $4 - z$ 6. $z + 3^3$ 7. $5(8 + y)$

8. $x + 5.7$ 9. $55 \div c$ or $\dfrac{55}{c}$ 10. $3y - 24$ 11. $y \div 6$ or $\dfrac{y}{6}$ 12. $\dfrac{7 - x}{10}$ or $(7 - x) \div 10$ 13. $(x + 9)^2$

14. $\dfrac{2d}{2}$ or $2d \div 2$ 15. $k - 10$ 16. $42 - (q + 7)$

3·4   O. 27   N. $15\dfrac{1}{4}$ E. -54 R. 12   P. 21   D. 41   S. -1.75 G. 30   A. -25 V. -27 governor

3·5   1. 52   2. 5   3. 2   4. -325 5. -32 6. -12 7. 28   8. 7   9. 41   10. -24.7 11. 27   12. 44

13. $\dfrac{2}{3}$ 14. 15   15. -20 16. 10

3·6   1. $3x + 5$ 2. $7t + 6$ 3. $4x^2 - 9$ 4. $6b + 1$ 5. $-2p + 15$ 6. $25q - 11$ 7. $12t$ 8. $15w - 5r$

9. $12m - 16$ 10. $11a + 14$ 11. $2\dfrac{1}{2}x - 13$ 12. $11n - 2n^2$ 13. $4x^2 - 10x$ 14. $25n + 4u^3$

15. $1\dfrac{7}{15}w - 4\dfrac{1}{2}$ 16. $2\dfrac{1}{10}y + 1\dfrac{3}{4}$

3·7   1. R   2. H   3. A   4. M   5. I   6. D   7. G   8. P   Diaphragm

3·8   1. $5(60) + 5(8) = 340$ 2. $8(-20) + 8(-4) = -192$ 3. $4x + 28$ 4. $2t + 10$ 5. $21 - 7b$ 6. $3(90) + 3(8) = 294$

7. $9(-40) + 9(-5) = -405$ 8. $4x^2 - 24x$ 9. $-2(50) + (-2)(7) = -114$ 10. $-6n - 18$ 11. $5m - 35$
12. $-12 + 3n$ 13. $3y^2 - 6y$ 14. $-7(-80) + (-7)(-3) = 581$ 15. $72 - 8y$ 16. $-14b - 2b^2$

3·9   1. $9 = 9$: yes   2. $-4 \neq 4$: no   3. $5 = 5$: yes   4. $7 \neq -7$: no   5. $15 = 15$: yes   6. $18 \neq 9$: no   7. $6 \neq -4$: no
8. $6 = 6$: yes   9. $-12 \neq 12$: no   10. $7 = 7$: yes   11. $17 = 17$: yes   12. $2 \neq 4$: no   13. $28 \neq 24$: no
14. $7 \neq -7$: no   15. $-19 \neq -26$: no   16. $19 = 19$: yes

3·10   1. $n = 7$ 2. $j = 48$ 3. $e = 16$ 4. $h = 15$ 5. $g = 18$ 6. $i = 49$ 7. $o = 24$ 8. $t = -31$ hinge joint

3·11   1. $n = 6$ 2. $m = 22$ 3. $x = 31$ 4. $c = 11$ 5. $y = 39$ 6. $b = 79$ 7. $t = 34$ 8. $n = 101$ 9. $m = 73$
10. $a = 76$ 11. $x = 110$ 12. $y = 183$ 13. $t = 44$ 14. $m = 91$ 15. $c = 205$ 16. $c = 106$

3·12   1. $k = 9$ 2. $a = 24$ 3. $n = 25$ 4. $g = 7$ 5. $d = 12$ 6. $e = 5$ 7. $i = 10$ 8. $b = 52$ 9. $s = 70$ 10. $o = 256$
baking soda

3·13   1. $x = 5$ 2. $t = 108$ 3. $y = 6$ 4. $x = 11$ 5. $c = 96$ 6. $n = 6$ 7. $x = 9$ 8. $b = 41$ 9. $n = 9$ 10. $w = 4$
11. $y = 2{,}916$ 12. $y = 900$ 13. $b = 49$ 14. $m = 8$ 15. $c = 63$ 16. $n = 121$

3·14   1. $p = 2\dfrac{1}{7}$ 2. $r = 13.46$ 3. $t = -8$ 4. $a = -7$ 5. $e = 11\dfrac{3}{4}$ 6. $o = 10.95$ 7. $n = -5\dfrac{29}{90}$

8. $s = -5$ 9. $w = 1\dfrac{1}{5}$ 10. $i = -4\dfrac{2}{5}$ inspiration; perspiration

3·15   1. $b = 1.13$ 2. $y = 1\dfrac{1}{6}$ 3. $x = -7$ 4. $a = 21.6$ 5. $m = 13.23$ 6. $k = 5\dfrac{3}{8}$ 7. $a = 3\dfrac{7}{10}$ 8. $r = -5.48$

9. $n = -32.5$ 10. $t = 36$ 11. $x = -10\dfrac{2}{3}$ 12. $d = 8\dfrac{8}{9}$ 13. $y = -14.1$ 14. $m = 49.1$ 15. $c = -18\dfrac{8}{35}$

16. $k = -3.53$

3·16 1. $n = 23\dfrac{1}{3}$ 2. $l = 10.15$ 3. $r = -59\dfrac{1}{2}$ 4. $e = 8\dfrac{1}{4}$ 5. $g = -60.48$ 6. $m = 2$ 7. $d = -5$ 8. $o = -3\dfrac{1}{5}$

Gregor Mendel

3·17 1. $d = 25$ 2. $h = -32$ 3. $m = -5\dfrac{1}{3}$ 4. $n = 6\dfrac{9}{14}$ 5. $n = 1.68$ 6. $p = -15.83$ 7. $x = -2\dfrac{2}{3}$

8. $m = 74.3224$ 9. $t = 16.08$ 10. $x = 1\dfrac{47}{69}$ 11. $y = 1\dfrac{13}{21}$ 12. $m = 19.53$ 13. $k = 41.36$

14. $m = -4.4$ 15. $r = 15.25$ 16. $w = -4.056$

3·18 1. $m = -4$ 2. $d = -9.1$ 3. $p = 8$ 4. $y = -11.125$ 5. $r = -10.8$ 6. $c = 87$ 7. $x = -25.2$ 8. $h = 9$

9. $t = -7\dfrac{13}{21}$ 10. $t = 98.6$ 11. $y = -2\dfrac{1}{2}$ 12. $x = -17\dfrac{1}{2}$ 13. $n = 63$ 14. $y = 158$ 15. $f = -150$

16. $k = 100.74$

3·19 1. $t = 10$ 2. $l = 12$ 3. $a = 8$ 4. $n = 128$ 5. $s = 17$ 6. $m = 123$ 7. $r = 216$ 8. $o = 9$ 9. $w = 169$
10. $e = 16$ Watermelon

3·20 1. $x = 3$ 2. $h = 30$ 3. $y = 6$ 4. $n = 1$ 5. $b = 24$ 6. $m = 6$ 7. $m = 32$ 8. $g = 175$ 9. $r = 7$ 10. $d = 0$
11. $c = 4$ 12. $h = 273$ 13. $k = 240$ 14. $x = 8$ 15. $t = 680$ 16. $k = 81$

3·21 1. E   2. R   3. R   4. O   5. O   6. E   7. C   8. T   9. B   10. R   11. D   12. R
13. E   Robert Recorde

3·22 Equations may vary.

1. $\dfrac{3}{4}(500) = x$; 375 students

2. $2520 \div 12 = x$; $210

3. $4x + x = 500$; $100

4. $36 \div 4 = x$; 9 inches

5. $4 \div 6 = x$; about $0.67 per can

6. $49.99 + 0.05(355 - 300) = x$; $52.74

7. $115 \div 5 = x$; 23 weeks

8. $7{:}40 - 15 = x$; 7:25 a.m.

9. $2(9.50) + 7x = 40$; 3 tickets

10. $89.99(0.5) = x$; $45.00

11. $n - (-4) = 8$; 4

12. $17 = 2c + 3$; 7 years old

13. $28 = 2n$; 14 computer stations

14. $219 = x - 25$; $244

15. $83 + 10 = x$; 93

16. $r + 50 = 215$; 165 pages

3·23   R. $x = 25$ I. $y = 8$ W. $n = 52$ M. $t = 129$ For S, T, A, and O, proportions may vary.

S. $\dfrac{3}{1} = \dfrac{x}{8}$ 24 caterpillars   T. $\dfrac{2}{\$173} = \dfrac{6}{x}$ \$519   A. $\dfrac{\$216}{3} = \dfrac{x}{5}$ \$360   O. $\dfrac{\$75}{1} = \dfrac{x}{4}$ \$300   two ratios

3·24   1. $x = 12$

2. $x = 6$

3. $y = 4$

4. $n = 7$

5. $t = 64$

6. $k = 72$

7. $m = 49$

8. $r = 139$

For questions 9 through 16, proportions may vary.

9. $\dfrac{3}{9} = \dfrac{27}{x}$; 81 parts

10. $\dfrac{156}{26} = \dfrac{x}{30}$; 180 pounds

11. $\dfrac{20}{1100} = \dfrac{15}{x}$; 825 calories

12. $\dfrac{3}{849} = \dfrac{5}{x}$; 1,415 calories

13. $\dfrac{156}{2} = \dfrac{x}{52}$; \$4,056

14. $\dfrac{5}{6} = \dfrac{35}{x}$; 42 hits

15. $\dfrac{2}{3} = \dfrac{x}{12}$; 8 boys

16. $\dfrac{3}{5} = \dfrac{x}{40}$; 24 dogs

3·25   M. 25%   L. 11%   C. 100%   P. 33%   K. 28%   A. 20%   O. 17%   R. 56%   Marco Polo

3·26   1. 100% increase   2. 67% decrease   3. 60% decrease   4. 150% increase   5. 13% increase
6. 33% decrease   7. 36% increase   8. 27% decrease   9. 53% decrease   10. 4% increase
11. 9% increase   12. 8% increase   13. 19% decrease   14. 4% increase   15. 11% decrease
16. 5% increase

3·27   H. $x \geq -18$ Y. $x \geq -12$ O. $x < -18$ T. $x \neq 3$ P. $x > 18$ S. $x < -16$ C. $x \geq -7$ U. $x \neq -3$
L. $x \leq 12$ A. $x > -16$ Staphylococcus

3·28   1. $y > 21$ 2. $d \geq 13$ 3. $x < 25$ 4. $t \leq 48$ 5. $m \leq -35$ 6. $73 > h$ or $h < 73$ 7. $-15 \neq n$ 8. $c < 18$
9. $k \geq -10$ 10. $67 \leq x$ or $x \geq 67$ 11. $t < 81$ 12. $y \neq 55$ 13. $-29 > r$ or $r < -29$ 14. $d \leq -72$
15. $w \neq 0$ 16. $p \geq 102$

3·29   A. $x < -5$ P. $x \geq 30$ R. $x > -5$ S. $x \leq -2$ Z. $x > 5$ E. $x \geq -2$ I. $x \geq -30$ T. $x \leq 30$ Spitzer

3·30   1. $n < -5$ 2. $g \geq 216$ 3. $m > -400$ 4. $-6 \geq d$ or $d \leq -6$ 5. $-4 \neq y$ 6. $c > -648$ 7. $-5 \geq x$ or $x \leq -5$
8. $y > -8$ 9. $k \leq 54$ 10. $-117 \neq k$ 11. $r > -4$ 12. $m > 5$ 13. $t \neq -84$ 14. $x < -1{,}156$ 15. $h \leq 21$
16. $y \leq -450$

4   Graphing

4·1   Inequalities graphed with an open circle and shaded to the right: E N W; unscrambled: N E W Inequalities graphed with a closed circle and shaded to the left: R K O Y; unscrambled: Y O R K

4·2

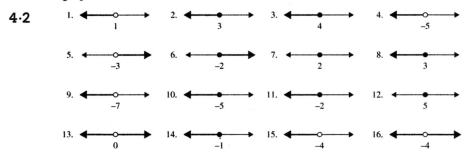

4·3   1. I   2. A   3. L   4. N   5. O   6. T   7. G   8. P   plotting a point

4·4   1. R   2. E   3. N   4. E   5. D   6. E   7. S   8. C   9. A   10. R   11. T   12. E   13. S
René Descartes

4·5   L. $\sqrt{34}$ V. $\sqrt{85}$ A. $\sqrt{106}$ E. $\sqrt{5}$ O. $\sqrt{68}$ G. $\sqrt{40}$ R. $\sqrt{8}$ C. $\sqrt{20}$ a locavore

4·6   1. $\sqrt{37}$ 2. $\sqrt{104}$ 3. $\sqrt{109}$ 4. $\sqrt{164}$ 5. $\sqrt{340}$ 6. $\sqrt{72}$ 7. $\sqrt{41}$ 8. $\sqrt{180}$ 9. 10

10. $\sqrt{52}$ 11. $\sqrt{106}$ 12. 1   13. 3   14. $\sqrt{34}$ 15. 7   16. $\sqrt{45}$

4·7   T. -3 S. -1 H. 2   N. $\dfrac{5}{4}$ L. $\dfrac{1}{4}$ G. 3   I. -5 R. 1   A. $-\dfrac{3}{4}$ E. $-\dfrac{3}{2}$ straight line

4·8   1. $\dfrac{1}{3}$ 2. -1 3. 0   4. Undefined   5. $\dfrac{1}{7}$ 6. 2   7. $-\dfrac{5}{3}$ 8. $\dfrac{1}{2}$ 9. $\dfrac{3}{4}$ 10. $-\dfrac{1}{2}$ 11. $\dfrac{1}{4}$ 12. $-\dfrac{4}{3}$

13. $\dfrac{1}{3}$ 14. $\dfrac{5}{4}$ 15. 0   16. $-\dfrac{1}{3}$

4·9   V. \$50 per hour   E. \$125 per year   T. \$15 per hour   M. $-$\$25,000 per year   Y. \$8 per ticket
N. 1 calculator per student   I. -10 points per test   S. \$2.50 per ticket seventy times

4·10   1. V   2. O   3. I   4. P   5. R   6. C   7. E   8. T   verticrop

4·11   #1 – 8

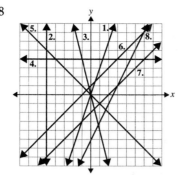

#9 – 16

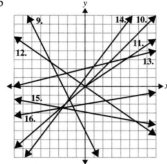

4·12   E. (4, 5)   A. (3, 1)   S. (1, –4)   R. No solution   H. (5, 1)   D. (–3, 6)   T. (2, –5)   V. (0, 2)
L. (2, –2)   M. Infinitely many;   have mastered

4·13   1. (1, 6)
2. (1, 5)
3. Infinitely many
4. (1, –1)
5. (4, 3)
6. No solution
7. (2, 2)
8. (2, 1)
9. (3, 4)
10. (0, 0)
11. No solution
12. Infinitely many
13. (3, 1)
14. (4, 1)
15. (–3, 4)
16. (–2, 8)

4·14   A. –1   O. 0   S. 10   N. None   E. 3   D. $-\dfrac{1}{2}$ Y. 1   I. $\dfrac{1}{2}$ F. 2   L. –2   Disney's folly

4·15   1. –1   2. 0   3. 1   4. None   5. 0   6. –4   7. 3   8. $\dfrac{1}{2}$ 9. –3   10. –5   11. 7   12. –8   13. None

14. 6   15. 2   16. 12

5 Functions

5·1   1. Function
2. Function
3. Function
4. Not a function
5. Function

5·2   R. 4   V. 0   P. 11   O. 1   A. −5   S. 5   B. −2   G. 9   Y. 7   K. −4   Garry Kasparov

5·3   1. 3   2. 0   3. 0   4. 3   5. 3   6. 1   7. 12   8. 1   9. −2   10. 0.75   11. 2.5   12. 0.5
13. −1   14. 27   15. 5   16. 5

5·4   1. S   2. 0   3. K   4. A   5. T   6. R   7. M   8. B   9. E   Bram Stoker

5·5   1. $(10, 5, 0)$

2. $(11, -4, -19)$

3. $(75, 0)$

4. $\left(\dfrac{1}{2}, 1, \dfrac{3}{2}\right)$

5. $(-1, 2, 5)$

6. $(3, 12, 27)$

7. $(-5, -3, 3)$

8. $-34, -28, -10$

9. $300, 192, 12$

10. $\dfrac{3}{2}, 3, 4$

11. $8, 11, 13$

12. $27, 108, 192$

13. $5, 14, 20$

14. $-13, -22, -31$

15. $1, \dfrac{1}{2}, 2$

16. $-1, -\dfrac{1}{2}, -2$

5·6   1. F   2. O   3. Y   4. G   5. N   6. I   7. T   8. L   9. M   10. A   Flying Tomato

5·7   1. $2x - 1$

2. $\dfrac{1}{2}x$

3. $x + 1$

4. $x - 2$

5. $3x$

6. x^2

7. $\dfrac{1}{x}$

8. $x - 3$

9. $4x + 2$

10. $8x$ or $2x^3$

11. x^3

12. $-x - 4$

13. $9x$

14. $\dfrac{x^2}{2}$

15. $-x$

16. $\dfrac{x}{2} - 1$